# SANDHURST

# SANDHURST
## A Documentary

Michael Yardley

HARRAP

London

For Brian, Dick, Nicky *et al.*

First published in Great Britain 1987
by HARRAP Ltd
19-23 Ludgate Hill, London EC4M 7PD

ISBN 0 245-54492-5

Designed by Millions Design, London

Printed in Great Britain by
R.J. Acford Limited, Chichester, Sussex.

# CONTENTS

# ACKNOWLEDGEMENTS

This book has involved the collation of a vast amount of material: many have helped. I would like to express my sincerest thanks to all those who have given so generously of their time and effort. To Dr Steve Badsey, my splendid research assistant, and to Dani Kaye who typed, typed again and retyped the manuscript I am especially grateful. My special thanks also go to my girlfriend Fiona Muggeridge who always knows where I've put things, even when I don't, to Chas Kiley whose skills as a photographic printer are evident in the photo-essay section (and to Tony and David for favours past), to the ever-helpful Dr Tony Heathcote, Curator of the Sandhurst Collection, to John Hunt, Chief Librarian at Sandhurst, and his colleagues Michael Wright and Kevin Jackson, to Jane Carmichael and her staff at the Imperial War Museum's Photographic Section, and to the staff of the Reading Room at the National Army Museum, to Bob Goodall, to Rosemary Baker, to Sian Rhys, to Michael Alachouzos. I also wish to thank everyone at Harrap involved in the project, including Nicholas Berry (who had the idea), the unflappable Derek Johns, to Tim Pearce and Helen Dunn plus the indispensable Roy Minton and Pamela Ruff; also Nigel Soper, Sandra and Ralph, the designers, who have done an extraordinary job under intense time pressure. I thank the Academy staff for all their help, especially Lieutenant-Colonel Willie Shackell, Major Malcolm Flower-Smith and my old friend Academy Sergeant Major Dennis Cleary. Last, but by no means least, I thank the Cadets, Officer Cadets and student Officers of the RMAS.

Thanks are gratefully extended to the following for permission to quote copyright material:

The extract from *My Early Life* by Sir Winston Churchill on pp. 44-7 is reprinted by kind permission of Curtis Brown on behalf of the Estate of Sir Winston Churchill. Copyright Sir Winston Churchill 1930.

The extract from *Memoirs* by Field-Marshal Montgomery on pp. 56-7 is reprinted by permission of A.P. Watt Ltd on behalf of Viscount Montgomery of Alamein CBE.

The extracts from *The Moon's a Balloon* by David Niven on pp. 64 and 65-6 are reprinted by permission of Hamish Hamilton Ltd.

The extract from *Bugles and a Tiger* by John Masters on pp. 66 and 68-9 is reprinted by permission of Michael Joseph Ltd and Carl Brandt, New York.

# SANDHURST
## A Personal Introduction

WHETHER one has been through the mill there or not, Sandhurst, or to be more formal, the Royal Military Academy Sandhurst, has a special mystique. It is a great and long-established institution in a country which values tradition; a rite of passage which must be passed by all the young men — and, in recent years, young women — who aspire to become Army officers. Parade Square or turf, Sandhurst is hallowed ground, and woe betide the author or journalist who doesn't tread carefully.

Writing a book on Sandhurst is therefore a project which I approach with more than a degree of trepidation. All the more so because Sandhurst is part of me. Atypically, I have been there twice; the first time as a fresh-faced nineteen-year-old officer cadet on SMC (Standard Military Course) 6 — a course which for medical reasons I never completed. My second experience was some years later, when, older and wiser, I returned to Sandhurst as a probationary second lieutenant on graduate course, D.E. (Direct Entry) 16. I had in the intervening years read psychology at London University, worked as a freelance photographer and been married. It says a lot about Sandhurst, and perhaps something about me, that I felt the need to return at the age of twenty-five in order to prove to myself that I could still 'hack it'. Sandhurst has a lot to do with proving that one can 'hack it', particularly as a member of a team.

However, I must confess that when I did eventually 'pass out' on 25 July 1980 I felt a slight sense of anticlimax, a sentiment shared by many of my contemporaries on DE 16 and by some (but by no means all) of the young men I interviewed recently. My own and my friends' sense of anticlimax was perhaps exacerbated by the fact that our course — in other respects rather similar to SMC — did not pass out on Old College Square but on the less sacred car-park concrete in front of modernistic Victory College. I am happy to report that the graduates now pass out on the main Square, an indication of their changing status in the Army.

Although I was a student at Sandhurst in relatively recent times, it has changed in many important aspects since I was there, not least in the arrival of female students. I have made every effort therefore, despite temptation, to ensure that this does not become a book about 'my Sandhurst' but rather a book which focuses on a Sandhurst soon to enter the 1990s. I have tried — although I have lapsed occasionally — to restrict my personal comments to the Introduction and Conclusion. All things considered, I think the book gains from my own experience. A complete outsider, unfamiliar with the language or geography, would have found it much more difficult to write, and had anyone wanted to, it would have been much easier to pull the wool over his or her eyes. My task in writing this book is to be as objective as possible. I do not set out to 'knock' or to write a recruiting brochure. I will sometimes criticize, but when I do it is in a positive spirit.

'I will sometimes criticize, but when I do it is in a positive spirit.'

Before progressing any further, I feel readers should be aware of the details of my military background. I do not wish to be criticized for 'sailing under false colours'. I resigned my commission. I did this in 1981, not long after completing my Sandhurst graduate course and, perhaps significantly, shortly before the Falklands crisis. I took what seemed a very drastic step because I thought that the Army was heading in the wrong direction, and, frankly, I had become disappointed with Service life. The regiment in which I was serving, and which formed the basis for my perception of the Army in general, appeared to have lost its sense of purpose and had become subject to terrible morale problems. After I left, I wrote about my experiences in the Press. I thought that the problems which I had observed needed to be openly and honestly discussed, and although I tried, I found it impossible to initiate this debate whilst remaining in the Army. I remain critical of many aspects of the Army, but then I am no less critical of the excesses of trade unionists, captains of industry or animal rights campaigners.

I have been impressed by many of my experiences at Sandhurst in the spring and summer of 1987. I was invited to go anywhere and see and photograph anything. I was never hindered, always encouraged. I have been on exercise several times, including once to Brittany, and on all those occasions was offered every possible facility, and usually with great enthusiasm too. That the Army should have allowed me such open access without imposing conditions of any sort is a very positive sign; few other organizations of State would take such a risk.

The method of this book is documentary; 'interviews', quotes and pictures make up a large portion of it. The technique is still experimental. I would be disappointed if I heard the finished product derisively described as a 'picture book' — it has a large number of carefully selected pictures within it, including my own extended pictorial essay on Sandhurst, but there is a great deal more besides. I have included some chapters of history, and have looked briefly at the other famous officer-training establishment, Woolwich, which merged into Sandhurst when the new Royal Military Academy opened after the Second World War. One needs to know something of Sandhurst's rumbustious past to understand its present, but the emphasis here is on today and tomorrow. Readers looking at officer-training or Sandhurst from a more detailed historical perspective are directed to the books by Hugh Thomas, John Smyth and Alan Shepperd, and the several excellent academic theses held in the Central Library.

Although it may sometimes appear so from outside, Sandhurst is not a static entity. Like other institutions, it may be fundamentally resistant to change, but it is constantly undergoing change nevertheless. The more important point is that this change has not always been as rapid or radical as some might have desired. However, this book is being written at a time when controversial and irreversible changes are being made at the Royal Military Academy with alarming speed. Periodic 'tinkering' with courses has been part of Sandhurst life for many years, and has usually been accepted by staff with resignation and a degree of humour. But the 'rationalization' taking place at the RMAS today has met with a great deal of opposition; critics have noted that change of itself is not necessarily progressive, it can become an alternative to true reform.

Writing about an organization in a state of flux presents practical problems. If I describe in detail a particular course at this moment, there is every chance that it might have changed by the time this description appears in print. This consideration may have stopped people in the past from using the documentary approach in a book. My way round the problem is to concentrate on what the young men and women passing through Sandhurst subjectively experience. I don't believe that this changes much from course to course. However, I have also taken a gamble in describing the more important courses in detail. I believe they will in all probability stay substantially intact in the foreseeable future. When they do change, one may be sure that they will not do so completely.

I have tried to take readers behind the scenes to see not just what the students think of, but also what the staff think of their protégés, and how they assess them. Seeing Sandhurst from the other side of the fence came initially as something of a shock. I discovered that the DS (Directing Staff) are really trying very hard to help cadets and probationary officers to pass their courses, rather than (as my friends sometimes thought), the very opposite! I have considered how the staff actually find themselves appointed to Sandhurst, and in particular the careers of those formidable men, the colour-sergeant drill-

'Seeing Sandhurst from the other side of the fence came initially as something of a shock.'

instructors. Although the role of the latter covers far more than 'square-bashing', drill remains a very important part of the Sandhurst curriculum. Indeed, in relative terms much more drill is taught now than before the First World War.

The RMAS is unique among the world's military academies in the brevity of its courses. Even with the recent one-term extension, the Standard military course is less than a year long (Territorial officers are minted in two weeks). This compares with a four-year degree course at West Point in the United States, or three at Saint-Cyr in France. Sandhurst has sometimes been criticized for producing amateur officers not suited to modern warfare. Now the trend is to 'professionalize'. More instruction, less education. It would be a pity if this were taken too far. A balance has to be struck between the needs of the student, the Army and society. The shortness of the Sandhurst experience and its emphasis on academic as well as military studies have been great advantages. Young men and women are allowed to adjust themselves to military life without having the spontaneity and flexibility knocked out of them. It also gives them more time to mature within the context and needs of a specific regiment or corps. The latter are not forced to accept as rigid or homogenized a product as in other countries. Sandhurst is not an end to a young officer's training. After he has completed his time at the RMAS, he will go on to a specific 'To Arms' course (whether to become a tank commander, an engineer or a catering manager), usually after a short spell of duty with his chosen regiment or corps.

**'A balance has to be struck between the needs of the student, the Army and society.'**

The flexibility which in the past at least has been a feature of the Sandhurst/British Army approach to officer-education pays dividends, when junior commanders evolve into senior commanders, or for that matter when they return to civilian life. It probably accounts for such things as our success in unconventional operations over the years. The 'square meals'[1] and other prolonged indignities the US cadets must suffer, on the one hand may encourage blind obedience and group solidarity, but tend by my own observation to suppress humour and initiative. Students at Sandhurst are still allowed to learn by their mistakes, and long may it be so. However, one must note that although this is generally the case at the moment, it appears that the advent of high technology (and the consequent rising cost of mistakes) may threaten this method of education in the future. Allowing students to make mistakes encourages a healthy, creative approach to decision-making under stress. If we let ourselves become the rigid slaves of new technology (and the manipulative 'management science' approach to leadership that goes with it) and banish learning by error,

---

[1] Where meals must be eaten using a limited and precisely repeated set of robotic movements.

then creative leadership may become as outdated as valves, and war itself more likely.

A disturbing trend at Sandhurst today, linked to the application of the so-called 'systems' approach (where the immediate needs of the system are the dominant factor in all administration and training) is that academic studies are being rather devalued. After the ROTE (Review of Officer Training and Education) report of late 1986 on officer-education a number of academic staff have lost their jobs or are in imminent danger of doing so. Some departments are to close, and all this is being done, it is said, to save money. That costs have to be cut in real terms may be unavoidable, but the academic side of Sandhurst has suffered disproportionate losses. It is a sad fact that morale among the educators is at an all-time low. Some of the most talented members of the civilian academic staff have sought employment elsewhere before the axe falls. Several have told me that Sandhurst will soon not be a military academy as such but merely an officer-training unit. I have given them a chance to state their case, devoting a whole chapter to what I believe to be a crucial issue.

Another topic of importance which relates to the above-mentioned debate concerns the changing career pattern of many young officers. The vast majority of Sandhurst students today join up not to become Regular officers, but on Short Service Commissions, to experience a few years of army life before returning to civvy street and more predictable employ. The Army feels that it may have been wasting resources on these entrants. In the interviews I have looked at the motivation of today's young officers — nearly all expressed a desire to escape the nine to five routine, at least for a while, and explained that this was why they joined up. It appears that many young men today view becoming an Army officer not as a vocation (as they once would have) but as a profession, an alternative to a job in the City. Nevertheless, while making such assessments one must never forget that a few weeks after passing off Old College Parade Square a newly commissioned second lieutenant may find himself leading a patrol on the streets of Northern Ireland. IS (Internal Security) training in general has become a very important feature of Sandhurst curricula. Terrorism and civil disorder are threats which are unlikely to vanish in the foreseeable future. How the Army sets about training its junior commanders — those most likely to face these threats at 'street level' — is a topic of vital concern.

The IS role has brought the Army into the limelight. I have examined how Sandhurst has responded by becoming increasingly media-orientated. In the newly expanded communications departments students are put in front of television cameras, interviewed and generally made familiar with the tools of mass communication. I

**'In the interviews I have looked at the motivation of today's young officers.'**

remember undergoing similar training, and have found it enormously useful since. However, I would also sound a cautionary note. I think it is a pity that today it is not so much what one is but what one is perceived to be that counts. The Army, it may be said, is well aware of this phenomenon.

Sandhurst appears sometimes to fall victim to its own image; it is perhaps inevitable that this should be the case. The image of Sandhurst has great continuity, and in its constantly evolving form outlasts individual careers. It may become overpowering, and is easily exploited. To the PR and advertising men, and to the Army itself, this is a valuable asset. For the individual who experiences the reality, though, it can lead to a sense of anticlimax and disappointment. I have already confessed that when I eventually passed out there was such a feeling and that many of my friends experienced it as well. That seed of dissatisfaction grew when I saw the rest of the Army in the cold light of day, rather than through the romantic gloss of recruiting literature. I would have been much better prepared had I better understood what to expect. The myth of Sandhurst and its development is an intriguing and complex subject, which to my knowledge has not as yet been given much attention. The danger, of course, is that people come to confuse, as I once did, the myth with the reality. This can have curious consequences.

**'Sandhurst appears sometimes to fall victim to its own image.'**

There are many more Barbour Jackets in evidence at the RMA today than when I was a student there; as a contributor to the Sloane Ranger books (and I probably shoot myself in the foot by declaring that) I never cease to be surprised at how influential they have been in stimulating this and other equally irksome fashions. Recently, a very close friend of mine, who still is an Army officer, was in all seriousness told by his adjutant that he should get a copy of *The Sloane Ranger Handbook* as a guide for improving his civilian dress sense so that it might become more 'officer-like'. I am delighted to say that my friend had the strength of character to put him straight by stating that the books had originally been intended as something of a joke, a catalogue of people and practices to be smiled at and not necessarily emulated. However, there is a serious point to this: it sometimes appears today that we perceive such trivial and easily mistaken (and purchased) tokens of class as Barbour Jackets, the right green Wellingtons or style of hat as equally or more important than values such as integrity and duty. It appears to be chic at the moment to resurrect superficial and often outmoded aspects of class-conscious behaviour while forgetting or ignoring the reciprocal responsibilities and obligations which were a feature of class in the past.

Sandhurst, which more than the vast majority of places in the modern world sets store on such old-fashioned concepts as honour and duty, has also fallen victim to this, partly because it has always considered — with the rest of the Army — external appearances as important, and, partly, I believe, because it has become slightly unsure of its role. While a great many of its students still come from middle-class backgrounds — the upper end of which may be said to provide the basic role model of officer life — more and more are coming from less socially advantaged origins, although academically or technically they may be well qualified. Sandhurst is in an awkward position. The British Army remains a very class-conscious environment.

It has always been part of Sandhurst's function to instruct would-be officers so that they should 'fit in'. But recently, as an increasing number of potential officer recruits come from working class non-public school origins,[2] the task has become more obvious and entails a greater allocation of resources and time. This can create problems; not least for the bemused young DS (Directing Staff) captains, who find themselves teaching a new subject, 'How to be Officer-Like'. Does it really matter what one drinks in the mess? What one wears? How one speaks? The Army would certainly seem to think so, and up to a point they may be right, but only up to a point. If the social origins of those entering the Army are changing, then perhaps the social practices of the mess should reflect this. This does not mean an end to tradition, or messes which look like motorway service cafés. It means we must allow new and relevant customs to evolve.

This book does not contain quite as much about the young women of the WRAC as I would have liked. Initially I found them less approachable than the young men of New and Victory Colleges, but perhaps this was due to my own inhibitions. The WRAC were certainly a bit camera-shy. My impression is that they are still a little unsure of their position. That said, they have become integrated into the Sandhurst scene with remarkable speed. One wonders how long it will be before one sees total integration. At the moment the WRAC are still trained separately, even though they march on with the male cadets and student officers during the Sovereign's Parade, and will soon wear a similar ceremonial uniform. One of them told me that she thought being at Sandhurst was much more 'prestigious' than being at the Women's Royal Army Corps College in Camberley. My own impression was that the apparent status of female students is still not as high as that of their male counterparts, but it is climbing all the time. Although it may be a long time before women are active in the combat role, it is clear that they are demanding and getting a much better deal.

**'The British Army remains a very class-conscious environment.'**

---

[2] In 1987 slightly over 50 per cent of all male Sandhurst students had attended a State sector secondary school, and 75 per cent of female entrants.

In conclusion, Sandhurst may be anachronistic in some respects but our culture is probably the richer for it. Unbridled 'progress' on so many fronts needs a check or two. There may be problems at the RMA, but compared with the despair and short-sighted greed of modern Western society, Sandhurst, most of its values, and the vast majority of the people there come off very favourably. This particularly applies to the students. I think one would be hard pressed to find a more personable and resourceful group of young men and women anywhere. This is their book, and I hope it will be useful and thought-provoking to them and all those who follow in their footsteps. I wish I had had something of the sort. I might have had a more realistic idea of what to expect.

In case there is anyone out there asking why 'that damned man Yardley' is scribbling about Sandhurst, my only remaining answer to them must be 'I am still fascinated by the place'.

*Michael Yardley.*

M.Y., KENSINGTON, APRIL 1987

# BEGINNINGS: 1799 – 1854

T HE ROYAL MILITARY ACADEMY SANDHURST, its predeces-
sor the Royal Military College, and the Staff College all ultimately
owe their existence to one brilliant and determined man, John
Gaspard Le Marchant, a Channel Islander of French Huguenot descent
who, as a British cavalry officer had a vision of an Army commanded
by professionally educated officers. The idea developed after his
experiences in the protracted war against revolutionary France.

At the end of the eighteenth century the British Army was in a mess.
Apart from those officers of the Artillery and Engineers who as boys
had been to the specialist school at Woolwich (see box overleaf), the
vast majority had no professional training. Officers at that time were
essentially aristocratic amateurs who often perceived war as sport, an
alternative to the foxhounds. Although initial commissioning and
further promotion were sometimes achieved by other means, such as
royal favour, the normal practice was to buy them. This led to some
curious anomalies, including ancient lieutenants and adolescent colonels.

During the disastrous Flanders campaign of the 1790s which led to
the famous rhyme being composed about the then Commander-in-
Chief, the 'Grand ol' (actually, he was only in his early thirties) Duke
of York', his own Adjutant-General, Craig, wrote:

'. . .We have plundered the whole country . . . we are the most undisciplined, the most
ignorant, the worst provided army that ever took the field . . . there is not a young man in
the Army that cares one farthing whether his commanding officer, the brigadier or the
commander-in-chief approves his conduct or not. His promotion depends not on their
smiles or frowns. His friends [family] can give him a thousand pounds with which to go to
the auctions in Charles Street and in a fortnight he becomes a captain. Out of the fifteen
regiments of cavalry and twenty-six of infantry which we have here, twenty-one are
commanded literally by boys or idiots. . .'[1]

[1] As quoted in *The Story of Sandhurst*, by Hugh Thomas (Hutchinson, 1961), p.20.

**Opposite:**

John Gaspard Le Marchant,
1766–1812. (*Drawing by J.D.
Harding*).

---

### WOOLWICH

In 1671 the Royal Arsenal was founded at Woolwich, and in 1716 the first two permanent companies (the equivalent of modern batteries) of the Royal Artillery were created and based at the Arsenal. The Royal Artillery required a higher standard of general education from its officers and men, particularly in mathematics. Throughout its history no officer of the Royal Artillery — or, later, of the Royal Engineers — could obtain a commission by purchase. As early as 1721 an informal elementary school was created at Woolwich and run on an ad-hoc basis for officers, NCO's and men of the regiment, but it did not last.

In 1741 a royal warrant was issued creating a formal Royal Academy at Woolwich to teach cadet officers. 'The raw and inexperienced people' were appointed to the Royal Academy on the nomination from the Master-General of the Ordnance, theoretically at the age of twelve. The course lasted five years and ended with a simple oral examination, following which the successful cadet was commissioned. In 1744 the Academy was reorganized and the cadets became the Company of Gentlemen Cadets, although their frequently rowdy behaviour might have led some to think the new title inappropriate. In 1752 they were housed in their own purpose-built barrack block.

In 1759 the Corps of Royal Engineers (founded 1717) whose highest rank was Warrant Officer, instituted its first commissioned officers on the same system as that used by the Artillery. Until 1761 engineer officers were commissioned into the gunners from Woolwich, and then transferred. After 1761 Woolwich formally accepted responsibility for training Engineer cadets.

In 1764 the reforming Marquis of Granby, the new Master-General of the Ordnance, sought to formalize the structure of the Academy at Woolwich. The Royal Academy became the Royal Military Academy. As well as mathematics, subjects taught included classics, French, 'the Art and Science of War' and fencing. Although entrance was still by nomination, a minimum standard of knowledge in mathematics and the classics was introduced, with the entrance age of twelve now more rigidly enforced. The first formal graduation examinations were introduced in 1765, when the Academy was split into a Lower division for boys between the ages of twelve and fifteen, and the Academy proper for adolescents between fifteen and nineteen.

In 1777 oral examination by interview was reinforced, and boys as young as fourteen were commissioned to meet the demands of the war in the rebellious American colonies. Even cadets who failed were sent to America, in the expectation that a commission would be found for them in some regiment. With the peace which came in 1783, the Royal Regiment of Artillery suffered a drastic cut in its establishment. Formal public examinations were reintroduced for cadets, but dropped again in 1793, only to be reintroduced yet again after the Peace of Amiens in 1802! The Woolwich Academy's famous nickname 'The Shop' is believed to be due to the workshops which had been part of the original estate when the Arsenal was founded in 1671.

---

Clearly something needed to be done. Le Marchant, who as a cavalry major had witnessed all that Craig had seen during the Flanders fiasco, was the man to do it. He returned to England, wrote a manual of improved sword-drill — he was a conspicuously fine swordsman — designed a new sabre to go with it, and toured the country with a cadre of instructors to demonstrate the new technique. This won him great praise and a lieutenant-colonelcy in the 7th Light Dragoons by royal favour, and with it a posting to Windsor.

With his new rank, and the knowledge of his Court connections,[2] Le Marchant felt confident to propose a whole range of improvements to cavalry training, and even devised a sort of prototype Home Guard as a last-ditch defence against Napoleon. Gradually he came to see, however, that whatever he did to improve the training of the men and the organization of the Army, the essential problem remained its officers. Improvement in their education and training became his obsession, and he directed his considerable energies to the task.

Whereas France had its academy at Saint-Cyr, Prussia its Kriegsschule and even Russia its Tsar's School at St Petersburg, Britain was without an institution for training its cavalry and infantry officers. After intense work at his own cost and in his own time, Le Marchant presented his radical plan for a British Officer School in early 1799.

He proposed an extended training system, far removed from the

Cadets lined up by their barracks in The Warren at The Woolwich Arsenal, about to leave for their summer holidays. (*Central Library, Sandhurst*).

---

[2] Even before his promotion to Lieutenant-Colonel, the poly-talented Le Marchant had been known to his monarch as a gifted amateur artist. A friendship developed between the two men which was to last until Le Marchant's death.

military school for boys at Woolwich, and subtly different from what was finally achieved. His new national military academy was to have three main departments and a supporting formation. The first department would be for fee-paying boys of between thirteen and fifteen who would receive a general education, but the orphans of soldiers would be allowed to enter without charge. Those passing the final examinations would be able (although not obliged) to go on to the second department, where they would study specifically military subjects up to the age of eighteen. On passing two final examinations they would receive their commissions without purchase. Thus bright boys of modest means would have a reliable course of entry into the Army without having to resort to the sycophancy and bribery that often surrounded patronage. Le Marchant's third department would be for officers who had already at least four years' regimental service, who would study Army staff work. To assist all three departments the institution would maintain a 'legion' of three infantry companies and one of cavalry, recruited from the sons of NCOs and other ranks, who would themselves learn military duties for three years before going on to their regiments with an excellent chance of future promotion.

General François Jarry
(*Drawing by J.D. Harding*).

Some years before Le Marchant presented his plan, a French émigré general, François Jarry, had arrived in England. Jarry claimed to have been the first commandant of the Berlin Kriegsschule and to have served there up to the death of Frederick the Great in 1786, although there is no record of his appointment. He had gone on to command a division in the French revolutionary army before falling out with his superiors, and had fled to England. Jarry, without knowing Le Marchant, had offered to give a series of training lectures to British officers on the higher levels of staff work. Although French expertise in this field was greatly respected, the former French general's proposition was not immediately accepted, but, in December 1798 the War Office gave Jarry the go-ahead, and brought him and Le Marchant together. A series of lectures began in May 1799 in temporary accommodation at an inn in High Wycombe. Twenty-six officers attended this first course, at government expense, under the title of Staff Training College with Jarry as instructor, and Le Marchant appointed as 'Coadjutor', with permission to recruit further instructors. A civilian was quickly obtained to teach mathematics. The lectures were intensely theoretical and all delivered in French.

After two rather uneven years for the course at High Wycombe, Le Marchant was able to secure the approval of parliament for his wider scheme. The proposal for the 'legion' was, however, too revolutionary for the time, and was dropped. Le Marchant was enough of a realist to be content with what he had achieved. In 1801 the government purchased for £8,460 an estate at Blackwater on the Surrey-Berkshire

The Junior Department of the Royal Military College parades for its annual inspection at Marlow in 1805 (*Sandhurst Collection*).

border and near the London-Southampton road to house 'a Royal Military College'. This slightly bleak and underpopulated area had once been the haunt of a highwayman who had turned out to be a local vicar. The Commandant's residence of today's Royal Military Academy Sandhurst is on the site of the old estate manor house. Oddly, the seller of the property was none other than the Prime Minister himself, William Pitt the Younger. Even more oddly, Pitt had just bought the estate, valued at £2,600, from the husband of his niece Lady Griselda Tekel. Pitt, whose genius in reorganizing the nation's finances did not extend to his own chaotic financial situation, probably made a profit of nearly £6,000 by his insider trading. It is probably no coincidence, as the historian and ex-Sandhurst lecturer Hugh Thomas points out, that Pitt had just been asked to repay a £4,500 overdraft by his banker Mr Thomas Coutts.

In the meantime teaching continued at High Wycombe with Le Marchant as commandant and Jarry as Director of Instruction. A royal warrant formally creating the Royal Military College was issued in June 1801, and in the same month the Royal Military Asylum (later to move to Dover, where it became the Duke of York's Royal Military

School) was founded at Chelsea. Intended to provide an education for the orphans of NCOs and other ranks, this approximated to Le Marchant's first department, although it never became part of the RMC. Later the same year the college was given a titular governor, with Le Marchant as Lieutenant-Governor and Jarry as Director-General. In March 1802 a further royal warrant created the Royal Military Cadet College (soon to be called the junior department of the RMC) for cadets aged thirteen to fifteen on entry. It opened in temporary buildings at Great Marlow, and by the end of the year had 42 cadets, all being educated at government expense. The pressures of the war against France expanded this number to 400 by the following year, but because of increased costs fees were also introduced. A hundred cadets, the sons of officers killed on active service, continued to receive a free education. The remainder was made up of sons of officers, the sons of private gentlemen, and cadets intended for the armed forces of the East India Company. The first year had also included a contingent of cadets for the Royal Artillery, but Woolwich had grabbed these back by the end of 1803.

The final achievement was therefore rather different from Le Marchant's original concept. The senior department, the 'Staff Training College', into which fees were also soon introduced, was composed of officers in their very early twenties with perhaps two years' regimental experience, and was physically separated from the junior department. The legion with which practical training could have taken place never came into existence. The senior department moved to Farnham in 1814, and it was not until after the war, in 1821, that it joined the junior department at the new Sandhurst site. The education of gunner and sapper officers had meanwhile been firmly retained by Woolwich, and in 1810 the East India Company, advised by Le Marchant, opened its own officer-training establishment at Addiscombe.

As long as the war lasted formal examinations for commissions rarely took place. The multiplying of training establishments, and the resistance to a single unified institution, suggests strongly that what was really being taught to cavalrymen, gunners and Indian officers respectively was how to behave in the traditions of their corps. Nevertheless, the RMC was a marked improvement on the previous system. The senior department, which by 1810 taught not just military theory but French, German, field fortifications and military drawing, provided all but one of Wellington's staff officers for the Peninsular campaign. But if the senior department was a success, the junior department presented the same problems of discipline and educational purpose which had long plagued Woolwich. To survive in either, one had to be tough.

In 1804 the RMC had suffered its first serious 'mutiny', resulting also in its first expulsions. The young and evidently over-optimistic plotters, who had tried to seize the armoury as a prelude to imposing their own control, received harsh punishment. They were ritually stripped of their uniforms, their swords were broken and they were barred by royal decree from any sort of military service for life. Despite such measures, maintaining discipline remained no easy task. The conduct of cadets and staff was criticized publicly, and would be again many times in following years.

In 1808 the fledgeling RMC became the subject of a pamphlet by one Pierre McCallum, who asked: 'Is not the Royal Military College more a seminary of vice, pollution and immorality than a profitable institution?' Actually, although there was some substance to his argument, it appears that McCallum had something of a grudge against the Army after being imprisoned by them in Jamaica. He used his attack against the RMC as the first step in a larger and more ambitious project. His next victim would be the Commander-in-Chief himself, the Duke of York. McCallum would be supported in his attack by a number of radical journalists and, in the shadows, the ambitious Duke of Kent, who coveted his brother's job as C-in-C.

Cronies of McCallum managed without much difficulty to get the Duke of York's jilted mistress, Mrs Clarke, drunk. She confessed what they knew already: before her rejection in 1806 she had been flagrantly 'selling' commissions by royal favour, and doing so at well below the normal purchase rate at that. A parliamentary enquiry was called. It soon became clear that York had been aware that the men being 'recommended' to him for the honour of promotion by royal favour were in fact lining his girlfriend's pockets, and that he had allowed her to supplement her income in this way as it saved him money. Meanwhile the staff at the RMC, still smarting at McCallum's attack on the college, published a counter-pamphlet in support of their institution and the Duke's good character. It did not do much good. York was forced to resign; his unscrupulous brother, however, did not become Commander-in-Chief; the post went to Sir David Dundas. The bouncy Mrs Clarke, who had amused the House of Commons by the forthright and saucy delivery of her evidence, became something of a popular heroine. She published a revelatory book and held back a second and even more salacious tome — containing her love letters from the Duke of York — on payment of £10,000 cash and £400 a year for life. Hell hath no fury like a woman scorned!

In the meantime the building works at Sandhurst were continuing slowly. At last, in 1812, The RMC Sandhurst opened. The junior department moved there from Great Marlow with 4 professors, 18 masters and about 400 cadets. The total construction cost had been about £360,000, of which as much as half had been creamed off by corrupt contractors. Le Marchant was not to witness the move. Promoted to major-general in 1811, he was put in command of a brigade of cavalry embarking for the war against the French in Portugal and Spain. He would never return. After an epic cavalry charge which had turned the day at Salamanca in favour of the British, Le Marchant, who might have rested on the laurels of victory, involved himself in a mopping-up operation against the retreating French. He died heroically, charging a French square. He had once written prophetically to his wife: 'Only death will stop me rising to the top of my chosen profession.' One wonders what this great soldier would have achieved had he lived longer.

While the wars continued both Sandhurst and Woolwich remained vulnerable to sudden changes in the demand for officers. In 1813 the first two companies of Sandhurst cadets, in the face of a shortage for the War of 1812 with the United States, were allowed to be commissioned directly without any qualifications being required. The demand for officers was equally stimulated by the war with Napoleon, but as soon as it appeared that this was over in 1814, the cuts began. The Army was reduced by a total of 220,000 men, and the number of vacancies for new officers changed accordingly. Six members of the academic staff at Sandhurst were dismissed, and the number of cadets dropped to 330 in 1818, and to only 180 in 1831. In the following year the Parliamentary Grant to the RMC was withdrawn. Henceforward the college was to depend on cadets' fees for its survival, and there

First Impression – a water-colour of Sandhurst's now famous façade by a newly arrived twelve-year-old cadet. (*National Army Museum*).

would be a drastic reduction in free places. A few years later, the War Office noted, referring to scholarship places at Sandhurst; 'it is doubtful whether it is desirable in time of peace to introduce officers into the army without means'.

A four-year course was being taught at Sandhurst which included drill and such directly military subjects as fortifications, topography and surveying. But otherwise it remained broadly academic, with cadets being expected to master mathematics, the classics, French and German, history, geography, English and religious instruction. The year was divided into two terms, and most cadets were expected to graduate by the age of eighteen. Conditions were spartan, discipline inconsistent and punishments brutal. Colonel Butler, who had been commandant at Great Marlow and gone on to become Lieutenant-Governor at the RMC Sandhurst, had, without Le Marchant's guiding hand, allowed a bad situation to get worse. On several occasions his students had literally rioted. He had abused his position to line his own pockets and further the careers of incompetent, but well-connected, cadets to whose families he ingratiated himself. Eventually the pompous and snobbish Butler was called before an enquiry at Horse Guards, but despite documentary proof of his misconduct he was not dismissed, although he did receive a mild censure.

Woolwich had suffered even more than Sandhurst after the general decline following the Napoleonic wars, and by 1826 had only 58 cadets. The age limit for entry was between fourteen and sixteen (raised in 1835 to between fifteen and seventeen), and in 1820 the Duke of Wellington was forced to rule that no cadet could stay at the RMA past the age of twenty, even if a regimental place was not available. In 1831 financial cutbacks forced Woolwich to introduce fees for the first time, although these remained on average about 20 per cent lower than those of Sandhurst in all cases. Despite economic problems, Woolwich was able to attract some very talented staff. In 1830, for example, Michael Faraday was appointed a master in the natural sciences, and continued to teach and experiment at the RMA until 1858. Woolwich fulfilled an important function in an age when science education was rare in universities and non-existent in schools.

Economic problems and indifferent government support troubled both Woolwich and Sandhurst for forty years after Waterloo, while in the Army colonels said openly that they preferred officers who had purchased their commissions as evidence of wealth and social status. Indeed, in a sense many of the young men from Woolwich and Sandhurst were the 'grammar-school boys' of their era. They were not typically members of the aristocracy (although a few boys from noble families did attend, and their presence guaranteed the hallmark of authenticity to the rite of passage), but members of the lesser gentry and professional middle class — exactly the same group for which the new 'public schools' were starting to cater. Just like the emerging public schools, both Woolwich and Sandhurst had problems with bullying. Horace Cockrane probably qualifies as Sandhurst's nastiest if most patriotic bully. During the eighteen-thirties he branded the initials of the King on to his luckless dormitory cohabitants following a Royal visit!

A decade later discipline had not improved and there was more public criticism. In *Dombey and Son*, Chapter 10, first published in magazine form in 1846–7, Dickens has his character Major Bagstock comment upon the RMC to Mr Dombey:

'None but the tough fellows could live through it, Sir, at Sandhurst. We put each other to the torture there, Sir. We roasted the new fellows at a slow fire, and hung 'em out of a three pair of stairs [a third-storey window], with their heads downwards. Joseph Bagstock, Sir, was held out of the window by the heels of his boots for thirteen minutes by the college clock.'

Dickens's fiction was firmly based on fact. The situation at the RMC

'Sponging for Credits'. Cadets and a professor at Woolwich in 1850. Sketch by D.G. Campion (*Imperial War Museum*).

Spongin' day for Credits

# Regulations
### FOR THE
## ADMISSION OF GENTLEMEN CADETS
#### INTO
## THE ROYAL MILITARY COLLEGE AT SANDHURST.
### APRIL 2nd, 1832.

1. The following are the Classes, and Rates of Subscription, upon which Candidates are admitted into the Royal Military College :

### FIRST CLASS.

The Sons of all Officers in the Army, under the Rank of Field Officers, including Surgeons and Paymasters; and the Orphans of Officers of whatever Rank in the Army, and of Commanders, and Officers of Rank superior thereto, of the Royal Navy, who have died in the Service, and are proved to have left Families in *pecuniary distress ;* to pay . . . . . . . . . . . . . . £40 per Annum.

### SECOND CLASS.

The Sons of Regimental Field Officers; and of Captains, under Three Years' Rank, and Commanders of the Navy . . . . . . . . . . . . . . . . . . . . . . . . . . . . . . . . . . . . . . . £50 per Annum.

The Sons of Colonels and Lieutenant-Colonels, having Corps, and of Captains of the Navy of Three Years' Rank . . . . . . . . . . . . . . . . . . . . . . . . . . . . . . . . . . . . . . . . £70 per Annum.

The Sons of all Flag and General Officers . . . . . . . . . . . . . . . . . . . . . . . . £80 per Annum.

### THIRD CLASS.

The Sons of Private Gentlemen and Noblemen . . . . . . . . . . . . . . . . £125 per Annum.

In these Rates (besides Education), Board, Washing, and Medical Attendance, are included.

The Sons of Officers who have voluntarily retired on half-pay, or *received the difference* in so doing, as well as of those who have sold their Commissions, are not entitled to Admission except on the last mentioned Class.

Two Brothers cannot be received on any Class together at the College, as long as there are other Candidates waiting for Admission.

The Orphans of General and Field Officers, and of Admirals and Captains of the Royal Navy, whose Families and Connections are not proved to be in such straitened circumstances as fully to justify their Admission on the lowest scale of Contribution, must subscribe according to the Rank held by the Parent at the time of his decease.

2. All applications for the Admission of Gentlemen Cadets into the Royal Military College, are to be addressed, by Letter, to the Governor, at the Institution, stating the Christian and Surname and the exact Age of the Candidate, and the Profession or Condition in Life of his Parents. But an application cannot be received, for the Registry of a Candidate, until he is ten years old.

3. No Candidate can be admitted into the Junior Department of the Royal Military College, under the full Age of Thirteen Years, nor above that of Fifteen. A Baptismal Certificate, under the Hand of the Clergyman of the Parish where he was born, if in the United Kingdom, or if the Candidate was born Abroad, such other proofs respecting his Age as may be satisfactory to the Governor, must be transmitted with the application for Admission.

4. Testimonials of Conduct, in the following form, must be produced within one month before the Admission of a Candidate, from every Master under whose tuition he may have been, during the three years immediately preceding :

"I do hereby certify that Mr._____was under my care and instruction, from the_____day of_____18___, to the_____day of_____18___; and that, during that period, I had reason to be satisfied with his general conduct and application to his Studies. And I declare, upon honor, that I never knew him to be guilty of any immoral or ungentlemanlike act ; and that he was not removed from my care in consequence of any misconduct."

Each Certificate, in this form, must also be attested and signed by the Parent or Guardian, as follows :

"I certify, upon honor, the correctness of the above Testimonial."

5. No Candidate can be admitted into the Royal Military College who labours under any difficulty of articulation, or under any other bodily or organic defect, which may appear to incapacitate him for Her Majesty's Service.

The 1832 regulations for the admission of Cadets into Sandhurst (*Sandhurst Collection*).

appears to have got entirely out of hand. The students were routinely engaging in knife-fights and other grievous breaches of discipline. Several articles appeared in the Press, notably in the *Quarterly Journal* and the *Morning Herald*. They prompted a fierce counter-reaction. Any reform of the military academies, it was suggested, might provoke revolutions and civil disturbances like those on the Continent. In 1848 a member of the anti-reform lobby published an article proclaiming:

> 'Why change a system blessed with such noble results? Or why, for the sake of crude theories . . . alter the constitution of an army which can point to a series of glorious conflicts, and noble acts of self devotion, unexampled in ancient or modern history.'[3]

That attitude would soon result in many unnecessary deaths in the Crimea. Indeed, application of the 'Now is good, new is bad' mind-set would hasten the deaths of countless young men in the Boer War and First World War as well. Once an institution has become accepted as part of the establishment, as had the Royal Military College by the 1830s, reform becomes increasingly difficult. It is amazing to note how often it has been assumed that because a system worked, or appeared to work, in the past, the same system will always work in the future — a curiously British attitude, and one which would afflict Sandhurst many times.

'Military Discipline', or 'Regs and Johns'. Johns were the juniors and Regs the seniors, whose wrath the juniors tried to avoid by fagging (*RMC Record*).

---

[3] *Naval and Military Tracts*, vol. 15, p.2 (Central Library, Sandhurst).

# REFORM AND REACTION: 1854–1900

O N THE OUTBREAK of the Crimean War in 1854 all military education had been suspended. In the first year of the war 95 of the 178 cadets then at Sandhurst were directly commissioned, together with 70 out of 195 cadets at Woolwich. Normally both groups would have had to pass an internal exam first; for the Sandhurst cadet this meant a testing in six subjects. Euclidean geometry, military surveying and mathematics were compulsory, but out of fortress studies, history, French and German one subject could be dropped. If a cadet failed he could still purchase his commission, and any Sandhurst cadet, whether he purchased his commission or not, took precedence over all other cavalry and infantry applicants. The cadet who did pass his examinations was commissioned at no cost to himself, which more than offset the cost of four years' Sandhurst fees.

Following the Crimean conflict, and the equally bad scare of the Indian Mutiny in 1857, two Royal Commissions and a Select Committee conducted a major investigation into military education and the workings of Sandhurst and Woolwich. First, in 1856 a commission was appointed under Lieutenant-Colonel W. Yolland to investigate Woolwich. Reporting the following year, the Yolland Commission was heavily influenced in its findings by its study of Continental military academies, visiting France, Prussia, Austria and even Sardinia. It recommended that the system otherwise universally in use should be adopted — that boys should be given a good general education until their mid-teens, and that only from the age of sixteen should they join a military college. This was, of course, exactly what Le Marchant had first proposed. The Commission was generally critical of living conditions and misapplied military discipline at Woolwich, and of the fact that the cadets had often no great incentive to work. It recommended in particular that the sons of soldiers and other special groups should obtain their places at Woolwich by open competition, after which their fees might be adjusted accordingly.

This was followed in 1857 by a Select Committee on Military Education which, reporting in 1858, made a number of important changes. The senior department of the RMC was broken off to become the Staff College — although it did not physically move to its new buildings until 1862. Responsibility for the structure of education at Sandhurst was taken from the Sandhurst Board of Commissioners, who had overseen it since its creation, and given to a new Council for Military Education. In 1857 the first open competitive examinations for entry into Sandhurst were held. They had been introduced at Woolwich in 1855; entry to both establishments had previously been by nomination of the Commander-in-Chief. The Select Committee also made the first suggestion since Le Marchant that Sandhurst should amalgamate with Woolwich. Free places were reintroduced by the creation of twenty Queen's Cadetships. These turned out to be a mixed blessing, since fifteen were within the patronage of the Commander-in-Chief and five of the First Lord of the Admiralty; the Queen's Cadet, who was required to pass only a simple examination on leaving Sandhurst to be commissioned, had even less incentive to work than his fee-paying fellows. Most importantly, Sandhurst followed Woolwich in shortening its course to two years and raising its age of entrance to sixteen. Both institutions therefore ceased to be teachers of young children. The Sandhurst cadets were reorganized into three companies.

Sandhurst remained vulnerable to any sudden change in demand which might be inflicted on it. Following the Indian Mutiny, the Army of the East India Company was absorbed into the Crown Forces and the Indian Army was born. As far as officer-recruitment was concerned, the Indian Army became the chosen destination of young men of lesser means because a substantial private income was not necessary. Addiscombe, the company's own officer-training college, closed in 1861, and Sandhurst was suddenly responsible for supplying officers to the new Indian Army as well. (Competition for the Indian Army became very fierce. To be successful, an applicant would have to pass out well.) Within a year of Addiscombe closing Sandhurst had been forced to increase its number of cadets from 180 to 336 and reduce its training course to one year, with a further six months for those who did not wish to purchase their commissions. Living conditions both there and at Woolwich, together with facilities for recreation, remained primitive.

The military authorities were slow to make the adjustments in

A sketch by Gentleman Cadet L.G. Fawkes of professors at the RMA Woolwich 1869 (*Royal Artillery Institution*).

discipline required by the change from school to college status. The results of this were two celebrated mutinies, first at Woolwich in 1861 (there would be another in 1868), then at Sandhurst in 1862; the latter occurred when cadets protesting about their diet occupied 'Narrien's redoubt', taking with them an 'inexhaustible supply' of stale bread loaves to use as ammunition to repel invaders! The mutiny of 1862 has become the most famous of the cadet uprisings, perhaps because it was only brought to an end after the personal intercession of the Commander-in-Chief, the Duke of Cambridge. After all attempts by the RMC staff had failed to dislodge the youthful conspirators, Cambridge (who had coached from London) made a lusty speech which was much appreciated by the cadets. They surrendered, having been promised by the Duke that certain of their friends who had left the security of the redoubt to negotiate with the RMC staff, and promptly been arrested, would be released; that they themselves would not be disciplined; and that he would look into their complaints.

The eventual military response to these problems was very similar to that of the public schools two decades earlier. They institutionalized the existing system of bullying by placing senior boys as under-officers over those younger than themselves (the military version of the prefect system) and they developed a timetable of mental and physical work which sought to control the cadet for every waking hour of the day. Still, when the unpopular lieutenant-governor who had been the focus of the Sandhurst mutiny (and a later riot) retired in 1864 he was not replaced, and the commandant became head of the college.

Reform might have gone no further than this had it not been for the persistence of Lieutenant-Colonel Lord Eustace Cecil, who in 1866 proposed in the House of Commons that a royal commission should be created to enquire into the workings of both Sandhurst and Woolwich, in the light of the wars in Europe and America during the previous seven years. This proposal was initially defeated, along with a proposal by Cecil for the amalgamation of Sandhurst and Woolwich. However, these proposals caught the attention of Edward Cardwell, the Liberal reformer. When Cardwell became Secretary of State for War in the new Liberal government in 1868 one of his first acts was to create such a commission, with Cecil as a member. Chaired initially by Earl de Grey — who was replaced after six months by Lord Dufferin — it included a broad mixture of politicians with military experience, Oxbridge dons and serving officers.

The Dufferin Commission reported in early 1869. It recommended the continued separation of Sandhurst and Woolwich, on the grounds that while the 'scientific arms' required high educational standards, the infantry and cavalry did not, and it would be unfair to penalize prospectively good infantry and cavalry officers by requiring of them academic standards which they could not reach. However, the Commission also noted that among the less academically gifted potential officers there was:

'a hopelessly idle element, composed of young men who, finding shortly after their arrival that they have no chance of obtaining a commission without purchase, lapse during the remainder of their stay into a condition of sluggish indifference, alike pernicious to the intellectual and moral tone of the institution. This demoralized and demoralizing leaven is still further reinforced by an adjunct in the shape of the Queen's and Indian cadets. These latter young men, having been promised a free commission on entrance to Sandhurst, without being required to pass any but a very low qualifying examination, have if anything, even less incentive to industry and emulation than the other class of students to whom we have referred.' [Report, p. 16]

The Commission was particularly critical of the overmanning at both establishments caused by the duplication of civilian posts for teaching and military posts for administration and discipline. It believed that the college would function better if the purely military element were reduced and more authority placed in the hands of the instructors. The Commission's recommendation that the Civil Service Commissioners should take over the setting and marking of entrance examinations for Sandhurst and Woolwich, as part of the civilian approach to education, was adopted. Its general view, that Sandhurst should be treated as essentially a civilian establishment for encouraging academic development in Army officers, has also been the view of every subsequent open enquiry into the institution, and has always met with no favour at all from the military.

During this period the purchase system had a pernicious influence on military education in general and the RMC in particular. Bridget Malcolm writes in her academic thesis on Victorian Sandhurst:

'Until the abolition of the purchase system in 1871 attendance at Sandhurst was optional. Candidates for the College were decreasing by 1859 and the competitive entrance examination system introduced in 1857 was purely nominal. Sandhurst cadets knew that if they failed in their studies there was always the alternative possibility of the purchase of a direct commission. Sandhurst did not guarantee free commissions to every cadet and it was not uncommon for idle youths to be withdrawn from the College to have a commission bought for them. The College could not afford to be particular about the candidates it accepted and often attracted the 'dregs' of the public school system. . . . The existence of the purchase system affected the whole role of the RMC. Because its function was not considered vital to the instilling of 'officer qualities', little importance was attached to its instruction. 'I think a man who has received a first-rate classical education, and has been brought up as a gentleman, makes a capital officer in the early ranks', Colonel Prosser told the 1855 Select Committee. It was the 'correct thing' to ignore all theoretical professional training.'[1]

Men like Colonel Prosser did all they could to prevent both improvements in officer-education and the abolition of purchase. They pointed to the potential dangers of a professionalized military, such as the one in Prussia (that argument would become harder to sustain after the evident success of the modernized Prussian system in the war against France in 1870). There appears to have been a fear (though it is rarely openly stated) that the country might be taken over by some sort of military dictatorship if the aristocracy lost their control of the military hierarchy. Purchase had worked well enough; why change? The Duke of Cambridge, the hero of Narrien's Redoubt but an otherwise rather intransigent Commander-in-Chief, argued vigorously:

'I should of course deeply regret any change in the system of purchase, for however theoretically objectionable, I think it has worked favourably in the interests of the service. It has enabled us to officer our army with gentlemen and it has kept our officers comparatively young in years compared to the other armies of Europe.'[2]

However, by the late 1860s there was a powerful and growing lobby which wished to see abolition. Their case had been well summed up by a would-be reformer a decade before:

'The reasons which procure commissions for boys desirous of entering the Army are various. One obtains his commission because he has a friend at court, another because he is a neighbour of the Commander in Chief, a third because his mother is a very agreeable woman, a fourth because his grandfather lost a leg at Barossa. But in no case are personal merits of the applicant considered for one single moment. Whether he is robust or puny, intelligent or dull, well educated or ignorant is never inquired. If he has 'interest' he gets his commission, if he has no 'interest' he does not get it ... No previous military education or training, no long and good service as a non-commissioned officer gives an applicant for commission in the British Army without 'interest', a preference over the idlest and dullest school boy with 'interest' who ever sought refuge from the Greek grammar in a red coat.'[3]

A Commission on the sale and purchase of commissions in the Army had come out clearly against the practice as early as 1856, noting:

'The system is vicious in principle, repugnant to the public sentiment of the present day, equally inconsistent with the honour of the military profession and the policy of the British Empire and irreconcilable with justice.'[4]

[1] Educational Reform at the RMA Woolwich and the RMC Sandhurst (Central Library, Sandhurst, pp.21–2.

[2] As quoted by Brian McDonald, in his thesis *Education Reform in the Military Colleges, 1856–1902* (Central Library, Sandhurst), p.32.

[3]and [4] McDonald, p.32.

**Opposite:**
A Pass Certificate for the Sandhurst Course given to Gentleman Cadet Edward Browne in December 1870 (*Sandhurst Collection*).

# ROYAL MILITARY COLLEGE.

*At a Board of Commissioners held at the Royal Military College, on the* 15th Decr 1870.

GENTLEMAN CADET *Edward S. Browne* having been found duly qualified to hold a Commission in Her Majesty's Service, at an Examination holden between the 8th and 14th days of *December*, 187*0*, in conformity with the prescribed Regulations, and having, furthermore, obtained from the Military Authorities of the Royal Military College a favourable testimonial of his general good conduct and proficiency in Military Exercises; We, the undersigned Commissioners, are of opinion that Gentleman Cadet *Browne*

is entitled to a Certificate, recording the satisfactory manner in which he has passed through the College course of Education, and do grant him therefore this Certificate accordingly.—

Although well-connected interests delayed reform for some time, it was eventually the needs of a rapidly expanding British Empire which would ensure it. Empire needed officers. Traditional sources could not provide enough, and so Sandhurst and the new public schools such as Wellington and Clifton rapidly became factories to produce the necessary imperial management.

Boys of middle-class background started the transition process towards becoming 'officers and gentlemen' at a suitable school, and the finishing touches could be applied at the Royal Military College at Sandhurst or the Royal Military Academy at Woolwich. The 'alchemy' of the Sandhurst experience became vitally important to an Army which would continue to demand, well into the twentieth century, that its officers appeared to have been born members of the ruling caste. It would be misleading, however, to give the impression that at any time during the Victorian era members of the working class had the chance to become officers; with the very fewest of exceptions, they did not.

When after the efforts of Edward Cardwell purchase was finally abolished by royal warrant in 1871 it was not, however, the instant success that might have been expected or as which it has sometimes been billed. The truth was more complex. Officers already serving who had purchased their commissions continued in their existing ranks, and on promotion or resignation were allowed to claim compensation from the Army for financial loss resulting from no longer having a commission to sell (the eventual cost to the State was £7,000,000). It took until the early years of the twentieth century for the last of these men to work through the system. The Cardwell reforms also created a new back door for commissions. The linking of the county militia with the infantry regiments of the regular Army meant that it was possible for a boy to be commissioned by nomination in the militia and transfer after a few months and after taking a simple examination into the regiment of his choice.

Cardwell abolished the old infantry rank of ensign and its cavalry equivalent of cornet. Instead, the lowest officer's rank would be sub-lieutenant (soon renamed second lieutenant). All commissioned officers would serve three years in this rank with their regiments as a form of probation, after which they would take an examination to be promoted to full lieutenant. Logically, this might have removed any need for Sandhurst at all. All prospective cadets, including those who had already paid for commissions, now applied to be sub-lieutenants and a surplus of commissioned officers over places in regiments resulted. The surplus officers were sent to Sandhurst by the War Office. Meanwhile any candidate who passed the Sandhurst entrance examination was at once commissioned as a sub-lieutenant. Many arriving at the RMC, therefore, thought it not worth working at all, as even the incentive of avoiding the cost of a commission had vanished. General Ian Hamilton, the commander of the ill-fated expeditionary force at Gallipoli, went to Sandhurst at this time, and he writes:

'During the year 1872, it was easier to shirk work and to get away with it than at any other period during the history of the Royal Military College. Some of us, like the Cavalry, were already commissioned as 2nd lieutenants in the Army; others were still more or less, in the school boy stage. No system could ever cover both lots effectively.'[5]

The problem was to some extent overcome when it was decided that marks in the final examination would count towards seniority after commissioning. In the final examination of the three-term, one-year course the top third would receive two years' and the middle third one year's seniority. Such problems did not, of course, afflict Woolwich, as it had never been troubled by purchase.

Cardwell's reforms altered the expectations of the better-off young men going to Sandhurst; Hamilton notes:

'We had hoped to be ensigns or cornets and to buy our way up to colonelcies as rapidly as our fathers' purses would allow — but here we were, going to be 2nd lieutenants on an even footing with those former non-purchase Sandhurst cadets — Dr. Benson's 'Hell over the Hill' lot — over whose heads we had meant to vault with the aid of a golden leaping pole. Many of those non-purchase lads were the sons of officers and every bit as well bred as we were.'[5]

Hamilton was not the first to observe of his fellows:

'They talked rather big. Everyone seemed to have been dragged out of grand houses, maintaining horses, dogs, grooms and gamekeepers.'[5]

However, General Hamilton went on to comment that the reality of Sandhurst life, especially for the newly joined, did not necessarily foster such delusions of grandeur.

'. . .Breakfast — a pint of milk for each cadet and bread and butter *ad lib*. For dinner at 3 p.m., a shoulder of mutton weighing ten pounds on each table of ten cadets, and ten pounds of what the authorities called plum-pudding — the cadets, 'stick-jaw'. The large lumps of suet found in it were known as 'Bagshot diamonds'. The beer, otherwise 'swipes', was said to be the water in which the brewers' aprons had been washed — but this is probably an exaggeration. The cadets at each table of ten had to drink it out of one pewter pot which was passed round; there was rarely anything left but a faint odour of malt for the last two. The cadets were allowed to make tea in their own rooms at their own expense but these were the only two square meals supplied by the State.'[5]

[5] *When I Was a Boy*, by General Sir Hamilton (Faber, 1929), pp.246 and 251.

**Overleaf:**
A timeless photograph of Old College and the lake taken in the late nineteenth century (*Sandhurst Collection*).

Although the entrance examination remained solidly based on academic subjects, the Sandhurst course (as befitted one taught to commissioned officers) was altered to become completely military in nature. Sub-lieutenants were taught six basic subjects which did not change significantly to the end of the century: Queen's Regulations, regimental internal economy, military accounts and correspondence, military law, tactics, and field and permanent fortifications. The sub-lieutenants, as we have noted, knew that they were already commissioned, and feeling that they should be with their regiments, had little incentive to work; while the courses, however impressive they might sound, consisted of little but sitting in a classroom reading a book. The living conditions and childish discipline were also doubly irksome to officers who could be as old as twenty.

It took until 1873 for the last of the cadets to work through the system, whereupon Cardwell changed it again! It was a feature of his reforms that he was willing to experiment and to fail until he found a satisfactory working solution. From 1873 all candidates for a commission — excluding militia officers — were required to study for a year at Sandhurst, and no nominations or exceptions were permitted. This is still, essentially, the system in force today. However, it is indicative of how little the educational side of Sandhurst was valued that from 1873 to 1878 the six candidates who passed highest in the entrance examination were excused the Sandhurst course altogether and allowed to join their regiments. Nevertheless, Cardwell's reforms mark a significant change in the status of Britain's officer-training schools.

Even as late as the 1860s, and though as yet they were a minority, it was extremely rare to find a Sandhurst or Woolwich graduate among the famous or successful generals of the Army. One significant exception is Charles Gordon, who passed out from Woolwich in 1852 (having lost six months' seniority and the possibility of a place in the Artillery after being reprimanded for bullying). From the late Victorian era onward the opposite is true, and it is extremely rare to find a famous general who was not a product of Sandhurst or Woolwich. Again, there are exceptions: John French was commissioned from the militia, having spent a short career as a midshipman in the Royal Navy, and Henry Wilson also joined from the militia after having failed the Sandhurst examination three times and that for Woolwich twice.

In 1876 the War Office took, by royal warrant, formal responsibility for education at Sandhurst from the Board of Commissioners, who were disbanded and replaced by the War Office's own Sandhurst Committee. The pattern proposed by the Dufferin Commission of an essentially civilian approach to Army education had been completely

reversed within ten years. Under the Sandhurst Committee's recommendations the RMC went back to its old system of cadets who were not yet commissioned or members of their regiments. The era of the sub-lieutenants had, however, left its mark. The new system, established by royal warrant in 1877, continued the one-year course in a general atmosphere more closely matched to a technical college than a school. The curriculum also remained the same, with little training in either academic subjects or practical soldiering. Rifle-shooting, for example, was restricted to a private club for cadets out of hours. As always, the system remained vulnerable to the sudden demands of war. During the new scare with Russia in 1878 a total of 110 cadets intended for Sandhurst were instead gazetted direct to their regiments, and for the 1882 and 1884 Sudan campaigns the top 20 Sandhurst cadets were directly commissioned without finishing the course.

For the last two decades of the nineteenth century Sandhurst and Woolwich enjoyed a period of relative stability which made the establishment of fixed institutions considerably easier. In 1875, rather mysteriously, the House of Commons went back on the Dufferin Commission by voting to amalgamate the RMA and RMC, but in the following year they changed their minds again.

The entrance examinations for both Woolwich and Sandhurst remained academic, requiring subjects such as mathematics, Latin, French and German, English history, drawing, geometry and higher mathematics; and the method of entrance was closely tied to the

**Preceding page:**
The Donkey Races, 1880 (*Sandhurst Collection*).

Defensive exercise for the Duke of Cambridge's inspection, July 1881. (*Sandhurst Collection*).

Forming a Square — typical of the obsolete tactics taught at Sandhurst well into the twentieth century (*Sandhurst Collection*).

public schools from which, by the 1880s, 90 per cent of officers came. Moreover, the majority of Sandhurst entrants were from the newer schools. In the year 1891 the long-established schools Eton, Harrow, Charterhouse, Rugby and Westminster accounted for 73 candidates for Sandhurst, whereas the new public schools Cheltenham, Marlborough, Rossall, Radley, Wellington, Haileybury, Clifton, Malvern and Westward Ho! (all founded in the middle of the century) accounted for 113 candidates. Of those boys the majority had fathers who were Army or Navy officers and only a handful, 8, were the sons of titled aristocrats.

Although the public-school system, cold baths and cricket matches, may have socialized a boy appropriately for his privileged role in life, it did not always equip him academically, despite special Army classes, to cope with the rigours of Sandhurst's and Woolwich's entrance examinations. A strange situation when one considers the Army and Empire were in many cases the *raison d'être* of the schools. However, deficiencies could be made up for at specialist crammers; the most famous of these was Captain James's ('Jimmie's') in the Cromwell Road. Fifty per cent or more of all candidates would attend such

**Overleaf:**
Bridge-building, 1897. (*Sandhurst Collection*).

41

establishments. Winston Churchill — perhaps not a typical product of the public school system, and certainly never the dunce he made himself out to be — nevertheless went to a crammer before passing from Harrow to Sandhurst. Churchill has left us his own account of his time at Sandhurst. It is worth quoting at some length. His sadness at the passing of that age comes across quite clearly:

'At Sandhurst I had a new start. I was no longer handicapped by past neglect of Latin, French or Mathematics. We had now to learn fresh things and we all started equal. Tactics, Fortification, Topography (mapmaking) Military Law and Military administration formed the whole curriculum. In addition were Drill, Gymnastics and Riding. No one need play any game unless he wanted to. Discipline was strict and the hours of study and parade were long. One was very tired at the end of the day. I was deeply interested in my work, especially Tactics and Fortification . . . I did not much like the drill and indeed figured for several months in the 'Awkward Squad', formed from those who required special smartening up. But the practical work in field fortification was most exciting. We dug trenches, constructed breastworks, revetted parapets with sandbags, with heather, with fascines, or with 'Jones' iron band gabion'. We put up *chevaux de frises* and made *fougasses* (a kind of primitive land mine). We cut railway lines with slabs of guncotton, and learned how to blow up masonry bridges, or make substitutes out of pontoons or timber. We drew contoured maps of all the hills round Camberley, made road reconnaissances in every direction, and set out picket lines and paper plans for the advanced guards or rear guards, and even did some very simple tactical schemes. We were never taught anything about bombs or hand-grenades, because of course these

The Riding School, 1881. (*National Army Museum*).

The Trapeze.

A Melée

The Horse.

Descent of the Masted Ropes.

Sword v Bayonet

Sword Exercise.

'Military Athletics at Sandhurst College', December 1881 (*The Mansell Collection*).

weapons were known to be long obsolete. They had gone out of use in the eighteenth century, and would be quite useless in modern war . . .

Horses were the greatest of my pleasures at Sandhurst. I and the group in which I moved spent all our money on hiring horses from the very excellent local livery stables. We ran up bills on the strength of our future commissions. We organized point-to-points and even a steeplechase in the park of a friendly grandee, and bucketted gaily about the countryside.

I learned several things at Sandhurst which showed me how to behave and how officers of different ranks were expected to treat one another in the life and discipline of a regiment. My company commander, Major Ball, of the Welsh regiment, was a very strict and peppery martinet. Formal, reserved, frigidly courteous, punctilious, impeccable, severe, he was held in the greatest awe. It had never been his fortune to go on active service, but we were none the less sure that he would have had to be killed to be beaten.

The rule was, that if you went outside the college bounds, you first of all wrote your name in the company leave-book, and might then assume that your request was sanctioned. One day I drove a tandem (hired) over to Aldershot to see a friend in a militia battalion then training there. As I drove down the Marlborough lines, whom should I meet but Major Ball himself driving a spanking dog-cart home to Sandhurst. As I took my

The filming of *Young Winston*, July 1971. (*Sandhurst Collection*).

hat off to him, I remembered with a flash of anxiety that I had been too lazy or careless to write my name in the leave-book. However, I thought, 'there is still a chance. He may not look at it until Mess; and I will write my name down as soon as I get back.' I curtailed my visit to the militia battalion and hastened back to the college as fast as the ponies could trot. It was six o'clock when I got in. I ran along the passage to the desk where the leave-book lay, and the first thing that caught my eyes were the Major's initials, 'O.B.' at the foot of the leaves granted for the day. I was too late. He had seen me in Aldershot and had seen that my name was not in the book. Then I looked again, and there to my astonishment was my own name written in the Major's hand-writing and duly approved by his initials.

This opened my eyes to the kind of life which existed in the old British army and how the very strictest discipline could be maintained among officers without the slightest departure from the standards of a courteous and easy society. Naturally after such a rebuke I never was so neglectful again.

My course at Sandhurst soon came to an end. Instead of creeping in at the bottom, almost by charity, I passed out with honours eighth in my batch of a hundred and fifty. I mention this because it shows that I could learn quickly enough the things that mattered. It had been a hard but happy experience.'[6]

[6] *My Early Life* (Thornton Butterworth, London, 1930), pp. 57–9, 63–4, 72–3.)

**Overleaf:**

The Gymnasium in the 1890s. (*Sandhurst Collection*).

The Woolwich Pistol Team, who have just beaten Sandhurst (1900). The Mauser pistol held by the cadet on the right in the front row was favoured by both Winston Churchill and T.E. Lawrence (*Sandhurst Collection*).

47

# THE TWENTIETH CENTURY: 1900-35

. . . When I went to Sandhurst we were not taught to behave like gentlemen, because it never occurred to anyone that we could behave otherwise. We were taught a lot of obsolete tactics, as in every army of that day; did a tremendous lot of useless drill; but never heard a word about 'responsibility', 'loyalty', 'guts', etc., because — so I suppose — these were held to be necessary prerequisites of gentlemen.

(MAJOR-GENERAL J.F.C. FULLER)

B Y THE END of the century Sandhurst had become not so much the modern training and educational establishment which Le Marchant had envisaged as a rite of passage through which suitable applicants might pass to become fit holders of the Queen's commission:

'. . .Young men, who although generally ignorant, were extraordinarily brave, unquestioningly loyal, blindly obedient and irreproachably well mannered in their own milieu.'

In 1900 the course taught at Sandhurst ran one year. It was made up of mixed general and military subjects, the majority taught by the instructors who were serving officers (there were exceptions — for example, French was taught by native French civilians). Despite the ongoing Boer War there was little practical military training, and, extraordinarily, still no rifle or revolver shooting at all. A competitive entrance examination was maintained, and there were further examinations at the end of each term. However, a cadet's ranking, which determined the regiment to which he went, was decided by his performance in the entrance examination, so there was still no great incentive to work. General Fuller remembers what sometimes happened during his military law class:

'Once a week for two hours at a stretch we sat in a classroom and read the Manual, and when we had exhausted those sections dealing with murder, rape, and indecency, we

either destroyed Her Majesty's property with our penknives or twiddled our thumbs. Fortunately our instructor was as deaf as a post, for this enabled us to keep up a running conversation, broken on occasion by a wild Irishman, named Meldon, banging on his desk to make our teacher look up. Then Meldon would solemnly say: "Please, sir, may I come and kick your bottom?" And our unsuspecting master, not having heard a word, would invariably reply: "Come to me afterwards, boy; come to me afterwards." '[1]

The Royal Military College Camp at Tidworth Pennings, Salisbury Plain in July 1903. (*Sandhurst Collection*).

The basic division of Sandhurst was into the Senior and Junior Divisions, but in December 1900 the Adjutant-General, realizing that there was insufficient practical work at Sandhurst (particularly in the ugly business of fighting) instituted a system whereby company commanders took responsibility for drill, PT, musketry and field training, leaving the educational staff responsible only for classroom duties. The college was notionally commanded by the Governor, who was deputized for by a commandant with the rank of colonel. In contrast to the relatively low rank of the Sandhurst commandant, Woolwich had a major-general. The RMA was organized into three divisions of cadets — left, centre and right — and ran a similar course to Sandhurst, but with a heavier emphasis on engineering and mathematics, and lasting for eighteen months. Woolwich, of course, still catered only for potential gunners and sappers. Other means of

[1] *Memoirs of an Unconventional Soldier* (Ivor Nicholson and Watson, 1936), pp.5-6.

getting a commission at the turn of the century were via a short spell in the militia (to be abolished in Haldane's comprehensive reforms of 1908) and by direct entry into a unit from university, although university graduates had the option of going through Sandhurst if they wished. In practice few did.

In 1902, in response to the shortcomings in officer-training revealed by the Second Boer War, the Akers-Douglas Committee on Education in the Army reported. It was particularly scathing about the expenses

The Sandhurst Chapel in 1907 (*Sandhurst Collection*).

involved in being an officer, and devoted a special section to the inadequacies of the cavalry. The Committee had very wide-ranging powers, including the authority to investigate whether Sandhurst and Woolwich should continue to exist. It reprieved both institutions, but its basic criticism was that economy had been aimed at, rather than efficiency, and that there was insufficient practical instruction. Its recommendations (all implemented) were for a stiffer entrance examination on five basic academic subjects, the raising of the age for entrance to seventeen and a half, an increase in the course length for Sandhurst to eighteen months and for Woolwich to two years, and the abolition of the post of Governor at Sandhurst. The committee believed that with the later starting age cadets should have completed their 'general education' (i.e., be literate and numerate) and that both establishments should emphasize training in tactics, languages such as French and German (qualification in one of which should become compulsory), and military history — although for years the latter had meant nothing but the Peninsular war and the Waterloo campaign. Officer instructor standards were to be raised by their serving no more than four years before going on to staff appointments — previously a posting to Sandhurst had been considered a dead end.

The committee was anxious that as little training as possible should be left in the hands of sergeants. However, their suggestions in this area would prove difficult to implement. A pattern had already developed at Sandhurst whereby NCOs had a considerable responsibility for the training of cadets. It proved too strong to break. The United Kingdom has always afforded a special status to its NCOs, and nowhere has this been more evident than at its officer-training establishments. Even today the responsibilities given to NCOs at Sandhurst would be unthinkable at the French Academy, Saint-Cyr.

In the years 1904–12 the Army suffered, partly as the result of the post Boer War reforms, an acute officer shortage. Unfortunately, it made a nonsense of most of the attempts to raise standards. The Woolwich course went up to two years in 1902 but was cut back again to eighteen months in 1909. Sandhurst instituted a two-year course in 1905, then decreased it again to eighteen months in 1906. This chopping and changing produced numerous problems; not least, a surplus of cadets over accommodation. From 1905 until 1911 an odd situation arose where one company of 'Sandhurst' cadets actually learned the Sandhurst syllabus while being billeted at Woolwich. Woolwich itself was almost empty of its own cadets. In 1904 the Woolwich structure had been changed slightly, with its three companies of cadets being given numbers and officially combined into a 'cadet battalion' under the Commandant. There was fierce competition for places at Woolwich. A cadet of 1908 has commented:

'There was no need (in those days) to advertise for officers, or offer them degrees to tempt them into the Army. For the Shop [Woolwich], especially, there was stiff competition for the thirty-five or so places available twice a year, and once in the Army, an officer intended to spend his life there.'[2]

Entrance to Sandhurst also remained by competitive examination set by the Civil Service Commissioners. Indeed, the situation was rather strange in that students had to work quite hard to get to Sandhurst; as we have noted, many had to go to crammers from their public schools

'Scotch-Up': an exercise in moving guns frequently practised by the cadets of Woolwich. The date is 1912 (*Sandhurst Collection*).

[2] Quoted by Alan Shepherd in *Sandhurst* (Country Life, 1980).

for supplementary coaching, but once they had secured a place the majority tended to rest on their laurels. Field-Marshal Montgomery, a Sandhurst cadet during this period, remembers:

'In 1907 entrance to the royal Military College, Sandhurst, was by competitive examination. There was first a qualifying examination in which it was necessary to show a certain minimum standard of mental ability; the competitive examination followed a year or so later. These two hurdles were negotiated without difficulty, and in the competitive examination my place was 72 out of some 170 vacancies. I was astonished to find later that a large number of my fellow cadets had found it necessary to leave school early and go to a crammer in order to ensure success in the competitive examination.

In those days the Army did not attract the best brains in the country. Army life was expensive and it was not possible to live on one's pay. It was generally considered that a private income or allowance of at least £100 a year was necessary, even in one of the so-called less fashionable County regiments. In the cavalry, and in the more fashionable infantry regiments, an income of up to £300 or £400 was demanded before one was accepted.

The fees at Sandhurst were £150 a year for the son of a civilian and this included board and lodging, and all necessary expenses. But additional pocket money was essential and after some discussion my parents agreed to allow me £2 a month; this was also to continue in the holidays, making my personal income £24 a year.

It is doubtful if many cadets were as poor as myself; but I managed. Those were the days when the wrist watch was beginning to appear and they could be bought in the College canteen; most cadets acquired one. I used to look with envy at those watches, but they were not for me; . . . Outside attractions being denied to me for want of money, I plunged into games and work . . . I very soon became a member of the Rugby XV, and played against the R.M.A., Woolwich in December 1907 when we inflicted a severe defeat on that establishment.

In the realm of work, to begin with things went well. The custom then was to select some of the outstanding juniors, or first term cadets, and to promote them to lance-corporal after six weeks at the College. This was considered a great distinction; the cadets thus selected were reckoned to be better than their fellows and to have shown early the essential qualities necessary for a first class officer in the Army. These lance-corporals always became sergeants in their second term, wearing a red sash, and one or two became colour-sergeants carrying a sword; colour-sergeant was the highest rank for a cadet.

I was selected to be a lance-corporal. I suppose this must have gone to my head; at any rate my downfall began from that moment.

The Junior Division of 'B' Company, my company at the College, contained a pretty tough and rowdy crowd and my authority as a lance-corporal caused me to take a lead in their activities. We began a war with the juniors of 'A' Company who lived in the storey above us; we carried the war into the areas of other companies living farther away down the passages. Our company became known as 'Bloody B', which was probably a very good name for it. Fierce battles were fought in the passages after dark; pokers and similar weapons were used and cadets often retired to hospital for repairs. This state of affairs obviously could not continue, even at Sandhurst in 1907 when the officers kept well clear of the activities of the cadets when off duty.

Attention began to concentrate on 'Bloody B' and on myself. The climax came when during the ragging of an unpopular cadet I set fire to the tail of his shirt as he was undressing; he got badly burnt behind, retired to hospital, and was unable to sit down with any comfort for some time.[1] He behaved in an exemplary manner in refusing to disclose the author of his ill-treatment, but it was no good; one's sins are always found out in the end and I was reduced to the ranks.'[3]

On the outbreak of war in 1914 most cadets at Sandhurst and Woolwich were commissioned without fully completing their respective courses. The practice continued, even though special short wartime courses were introduced at both establishments. Immediately the war began the Sandhurst course was reduced to only three months, but by the end of 1915 this was lengthened to six months, although in practice many cadets were commissioned early. In 1916 the course was extended to eight months, and by the next year it had grown yet again, to ten months. By the last year of the war, it ran a full year. Alan Shepperd, in his history of Sandhurst, has pointed out:

'The length of any one course was in reality tied to the constantly changing war situation and the often sudden and urgent need to find more and more officers, not only for the Western Front with its appalling casualties, but for the growing number of overseas theatres of war.'

He later quotes a cadet who joined in January 1918:

'We were drilled and drilled and had lots of riding, gym and rifle instruction, together with elementary tactics, but I don't remember doing much digging. We were taught law up to courts martial and administration up to battalion level. We started at 6 a.m. and worked all day, and with lectures after mess, this took us up to 11 p.m. The atmosphere was that life was going to be short.'[4]

Tragically, for a huge number of those at both Sandhurst and Woolwich, it was. (During the 1914–18 period Woolwich ran similar shortened courses to those at Sandhurst but with a more technical orientation). When the armistice came over four thousand Sandhurst cadets alone had perished in the War to end all Wars. Thirty-seven had won the Victoria Cross.

[3]*Memoirs* (Collins, 1958), pp. 23-5. There is no confirmation of Montgomery's account in the Sandhurst records, and some historians have therefore questioned it.

[4] *Sandhurst*, pp. 122 and 126.

**Overleaf:**
About to be launched into the maelström: A Sandhurst Company in 1916 (*Sandhurst Collection*).

"B" Company, Revue, JULY 28th, 1918. R. M. C.

A playbill for a summer revue by "B" Company of the Royal Military College, July 1918 (*Sandhurst Collection*).

In 1920 both Sandhurst and Woolwich were reconstituted as before, but each with a two-year course. Officers of the new Royal Tank Corps could attend either establishment. Also that year the old ten companies at Sandhurst were amalgamated into five, embodied like Woolwich in a 'cadet battalion' under the commandant. Additional academic papers of military history and the history and geography of the Empire were introduced into the syllabus. In 1922 fees were revised, so that while most fathers paid about £200 a year for their sons to attend Sandhurst, sons of Army officers paid on a sliding scale down to about a quarter of that amount. King's Cadets, and some King's Indian Cadets, were exempt from fees. Also in 1922 Sandhurst took its first NCO for commission. These men were required to be under twenty-four and unmarried, and took a one-year course, being known as 'Y-Cadets'.

In June 1923 the Haldane Committee (under the great pre-war reformer, Lord Haldane) produced its report, which set the pattern for

Cadets cheer at athletics meeting, Sandhurst 1919. (*Topham*).

The first Indian and Burmese cadets for entry to RMC Sandhurst at the Examining Board, Simla 1920. (*Sandhurst Collection*).

Sandhurst and Woolwich until the Second World War. The committee expressed a fear that the 'premature arrest of intellectual development' might deprive the Army of competent leaders later in their careers. It recommended the relaxing of purely military discipline at Sandhurst and Woolwich, and increasing the amount of general education, while reducing the length of the course at both to eighteen months. The average age of cadets on entry would rise to eighteen. The two institutions would teach the same basic syllabus, with a greater emphasis at Woolwich on mathematics and science. Most of the teaching was in theory to be by civilian staff, although thanks to economy measures company commanders might throughout the 1930s be required to teach subjects of which they knew nothing. From this basic course gunners would go on to a three-month extension course at Larkhill, and sappers to a two-year course at Cambridge University and Chatham School of Military Engineering.

In 1924 Army Council scholarships were created, and six were set up at Sandhurst. The remaining changes through to 1939 were minor, and made against a background of economy measures, officer shortages, and general apathy. Lord Belhaven, who joined Sandhurst in 1924, recalls:

'For years of the Great War, soldiering had been a national profession and the nation was tired of it. The Army lacked everything but human quality — officers, men and equipment. Men who wanted to make a success of life did not apply for commissions; ten shillings and sixpence a day in an expensive mess was penury. In most regiments of the line and in the Royal Artillery such things as tennis racquets and cricket bats were shared; it was no wonder that few Sandhurst cadets applied for leave outside the Aldershot district; they had little money to spare. The regiment which I hoped to join, the Royal Scots Fusiliers, was then an expensive one; but it had shortly to cut expenses to the bone, to allow the sons of its former officers to join it. It was the same everywhere, even to a certain extent in the Brigade of Guards and the cavalry. The politicians promised to 'make soldiering a career', but, like most of their promises, this one was not kept, and, as the cost of living rose, officers' pay was cut. They cared nothing for us, we had few votes, and to cut down on 'officer class' added to the popularity on which their livelihood depended.'[5]

In 1928 both Woolwich and Sandhurst received their first cadets come up through the ranks. It was all the more inevitable because there simply were not enough members of the middle and upper classes coming forward; thus as imperial necessity had brought the middle class into the Army, economic decline in the context of the needs of the same increasingly burdensome Empire helped to open the door for the working class.

Despite the general mood towards economy, one area of training which carried on as ever at both Woolwich and Sandhurst was horsemanship. Indeed, it was one of the few parts of the Sandhurst

A VIP visits Sandhurst in the late 1920s.

curriculum, apart from drill, taken really seriously by cadets and staff alike. Back to Lord Belhaven:

Equitation at Sandhurst in the 1930s (*Sandhurst Collection*)

'The riding and management of horses was a subject of great importance in the Army in those days. In France and Flanders, cavalry had not been used on any scale after the Battle of the Marne; even Le Cateau had been fought dismounted. But cavalry, under a cavalry general, had conquered Palestine and Syria and they still held Transjordan and Iraq. For the infantryman, the horse was all-important. It carried his reconnaissance parties, it pulled his machine-guns, his ammunition, his rations and his cookers. Every infantry battalion had fifteen mounted officers and every officer had to be able to sit on a horse, steer it about, know how to feed it and how to treat it for diseases and injuries. Every Sandhurst cadet had therefore to learn how to ride in some fashion and how to manage horses. Sharp-tongued, with their high-pitched cavalry voices, the riding staff threw themselves into their unequal task, while the horses threw us about the country-side. I held a record in equitation for falling off nine times in an hour, my final descent being on an obstacle known as the Cheveaux de Frise, an open ditch, filled with wooden sharp stakes. "Cor!" exclaimed Woodward. "Look at Mr. Bel'aven sittin' in the Chevoo de Frise!" My horse, Bruiser, looked at me also, and sighed hopelessly.'[5]

Cadets were organized into a number of rides depending on their ability. The most advanced was for those who had hunted, the most basic for those with no knowledge of horses at all. As far as the internal combustion engine was concerned there was no instruction,

[5] As quoted by Hugh Thomas, *The Story of Sandhurst* (Hutchinson, 1961), pp.184-5.

although Woolwich would introduce a course in car-maintenance in 1931.

During the late twenties the RMC had one of its most famous adjutants, Major 'Boy' Browning, of the Grenadier Guards (he later married the novelist Daphne du Maurier, and as a lieutenant-general in the Second World War commanded British Airborne Forces) and one of its most famous NCOs, the legendary Sergeant-Major Brittain. A cadet member of the sergeant-major's Sandhurst company was none other than David Niven. Appropriately, Niven, who would so often play the archetypal British officer, had a distinguished Sandhurst career, becoming an under-officer (the Sandhurst equivalent of a senior prefect) and a member of the rugger team, David Niven has made some very perceptive comments on the Sandhurst system in his enthralling about-to-be-filmed autobiography *The Moon's a Balloon*. New cadets, he explains, were initiated into the RMC via the drill square:

'The 'mud treatment' started on the first day of our ten weeks of concentrated drill 'on the square'. We were paraded in the civilian clothes in which we had arrived the day before . . . Quickly and efficiently we were stripped of umbrellas and walking sticks and shown how to come to attention, how to march and how to halt. Then, at a hair-raising speed we were marched one and a half miles to be issued with boots and canvas uniforms. Round and round the College we whizzed, sweating and apprehensive beneath the patronising glances of beautifully turned out older cadets to the barbers to be shorn like sheep, to the gym to be fitted with physical training outfits, to the stables for breeches, brown boots and leggings, to the laundry 'because I don't want to see a speck of dirt for the next year an' 'arf mind' and finally to the Chapel 'because 'ere, gentlemen, you can thank Almighty Gawd at the end of each week if you are still breathin'. Got it?' 'GOT IT STAFF!'. . .

Normally, there were fifteen minutes between being dismissed from one parade and being inspected for the next in a totally different and spotless outfit. The slightest lapse, a finger mark on a brass button, a cap at the wrong angle or hair not mown like a convict was rewarded with the 'Defaulters' — a particularly gruelling extra drill in full battle order at the end of the day when everyone else was resting . . .

. . .The great thing about those first ten weeks was that although one was being treated like mud, it was at least grown-up mud. We were treated like men for the first time in our lives and as men we were expected to react.'[6]

A classic Niven story even if it is apocryphal (much of Sandhurst history is!), concerns his time as 'Commandant's Orderly'. To fulfil in spirit the requirements of this sober ceremonial office, he was in the habit of carrying certain special-affairs supplies in the ornate message box on his cross-belt. One day the general, having heard rumours, decided to surprise his two orderlies with an inspection:

Hore-Belisha inspects a Woolwich cadet practising gas drill in the late 1930s. (*Keystone*).

'We immediately sprang to attention secure and relaxed in the knowledge that we too were faultlessly turned out. I was on Dick's right, so the General looked first at my cap, chin, my buttons, my belt, my creases and my boots. Then, with a pace to the side and in the usual army fashion, he started on Dick from his boots to his cap. Round the back he went, inspecting Dick from the rear when Christ! I heard a little click as he opened Dick's Message Box.

The joke of what mine contained had long since been over, hardly anybody bothered to ask me any more what was in it — everyone knew — in fact I had forgotten all about it

65

myself. The few seconds that it took the Commander to inspect Dick's rear view seemed to me to take until autumn. Finally, I heard his breathing directly behind me. I prayed he would move round to the front again without looking into my box. I promised God all sorts of rash things if he would arrange this for me, but he failed me. I felt rather than heard the General open my Box and I sensed him rustling about among its horrible contents — Woodbines, matches, lavatory paper and French letters! My military career was obviously over before it had even started and I toyed with the idea of falling on my bayonet among the rhododendron petals. Dick too had realised the full possibilities of the situation and started to vibrate like a harp-string on my left, a condition brought about by a mixture of concern for his partner, suppressed laughter and keen anticipation of impending doom.

After an eternity, Major-General Sir Eric Girdwood stood before me. He looked for a long time at my sea-green face without saying a word. Staring blankly ahead, I waited for the axe to fall.

"Niven," he said, "I had heard about that . . . thank you very much . . . you are very considerate. . ." '[6]

Despite the activities of Cadet Under-Officer Niven the years of the depression were hard ones for Sandhurst. The cost to the State of educating a cadet at the RMC was only £550, yet there was pressure for further economy. Sandhurst even cut food rations to cadets. Amalgamation between Sandhurst and Woolwich might have been one way of cutting costs, but both institutions managed to survive as separate entities up till the outbreak of the Second World War. The writer John Masters has left in his memoirs a very detailed account of Sandhurst life in the early thirties;[7] apart from the brutality and cheating mentioned, much of his description could apply to Sandhurst today:

'We learned one another's names and faces and what schools we had come from. We found our way to the fancy goods store — the F.G.S., or Jesus — to buy cigarettes and cups of tea and buns. We sat down to meals at long, polished tables, and used our new freedom to order bottles of Tollemache beer and glasses of port. The mess waiters, who were also the room servants, hovered over us, wearing mixed expressions of tolerant affection and cynical scorn. They were all ex-soldiers and most of them had seen twenty or thirty batches of us arrive, learn, conform, pass on.

We learned the grades of the hierarchy. In the clouds lived a major-general, the commandant, whom we seldom saw after the first Sunday, when he gave us a talk on sex. Some day we were going to hope to be worthy of the love of a good woman, he said; that thought should guide us while we were here at the R.M.C. (Yes, but how can you recognize a good woman when you don't know anything about bad women? There was a lot to find out.) . . .

[6] From *The Moon's a Balloon*, by David Niven (Hamish Hamilton, 1971), pp. 57-9, 61-3 (Coronet edition).

Between parades we had five or ten minutes to change clothes and be on parade again, always spotless, puttees tightly tied. We learned the techniques of frantic hurry. We learned to stand still. Every morning at dawn they held a shaving parade, ostensibly to see whether we were properly dressed and shaved but in reality to order us to have another haircut. I had my hair cut three times in one week.

The lordly Adjutant, beautiful beyond belief with his dark blue hat, red face, glossy boots, and golden spurs, strode slowly around among our scurrying squads, communing in silent scorn with some Coldstream deity who hovered a hundred feet up in the air in front of him. Before his feet steps became level ramps, doors opened, potholes were filled, walls vanished. He never tripped or stumbled and he never looked down, round or about. Everyone else senior to us — that is, everyone — looked at us as if we were mutinous lice and on the occasion of the smallest misdemeanour would mutter, drawl or shout, 'Take his name.' From somewhere behind us an answering voice would instantly bawl, 'Gottim, sir.' Maybe the sergeant hadn't got him, but he scribbled fiercely on a pad and usually found out in the end whose name he should have written down. For serious offences, such as having a button undone, the cry was, 'Puttim in the guard-room' — that is, under close arrest. Again the yell went up, 'Gottim, sir,' and the recreant was rushed off, between a couple of sergeants, up the great steps into the guard-room. . .

The word 'idle' meant anything that the staff considered unsoldierly. We *were* idle; we *had* idle haircuts, idle rifles, idle bicycles; we *did* idle salutes, idle jumps . . . for nine weeks the drill parades seemed to be continuous . . . I know we went occasionally to the class rooms and the gymnasium; but I can remember only the square . . .

Gradually the desperate pace slackened. The staff, having reduced us in drill matters to cataleptic automata, started working up our self-confidence on that foundation. Their new attitude could never have been called cosy but a mistake was recorded with a brusque word instead of a spine-curdling shriek. . . At last we passed off the square at an inspection held by officers from the depot of the Brigade of Guards at Caterham . . .

We settled into the normal pattern of the R.M.C. The number of drill parades decreased, though they were still many. Academic work increased, and we were permitted to join the rest of the company on Adjutant's parade every Saturday and church parade every Sunday. We were allowed late leave and took trips to Aldershot on our bicycles to go to the flicks. On Saturdays we went to London by bus and there savoured the delights of the wicked capital . . .

Cliques formed, the most noticeable being the foxhunting set, who spent a lot of time tearing down the long corridors, blowing hunting horns. This clique wore riding clothes whenever possible . . . There was ill feeling, and one crowd murmured, 'The unspeakable in pursuit of the uneatable,' and the other crowd cheered, 'Oiks!' . . .

We all acquired the right clothes. These were: grey flannel trousers, a doggy tweed coat with skirts to the knees and two slits at the back, a tweed gorblimey cap worn well forward on the head, the peak sewn down to the rim of the brim. In this garb we were recognisable a mile off as Gentlemen Cadets, and a good thing too. We never wore uniforms off the grounds of the R.M.C. . . .

We came from every level of British society . . . One young Lord was sent a bottle of brandy and half a dozen pints of champagne every week by the peer his father . . . At the

**Preceding page:**
French reserve officers on a
visit to Sandhurst just before
the Second World War.

other end of the social scale there were some young men from the lower - middle and working classes. These had enlisted in the ranks, had there been selected as officer material and had been sent to the R.M.C. as 'A' (for Army) cadets. Of course they varied as much as the aristocrats, the brewers or the bourgeosie, but this was a considerable discovery to most of us, for we had never before been exposed to such people on equal terms.

The Master of Wellington, which was only a few miles away, had once caused a great uproar by referring to the R.M.C. as 'the little hell over the hill' . . . The R.M.C. was undoubtedly brutal, and it was an 'A' cadet who was the occasion of my introduction to this notorious fact.

This particular man, several years older than the rest of us, let it be known that he had played rugby football for the Army and was, besides, a heavyweight boxer of repute. It immediately became apparent that he had seldom played rugger and was a coward into the bargain . . . That evening I heard a lot of gasping and banging in the corridor and went out to find a gang of G.C.s breaking up the would-be hero's room and shaving off half his luxuriant moustache . . . They were trying to show the liar that the code of one's circle, whatever it may be, can be transgressed only by men who are prepared to take the consequences. The victim didn't heed the lesson, which might have been cheaply learned at the cost of a few bruises and half a moustache. I saw his name in the *News of the World* some time later. He was getting seven years for bigamy . . .

At the R.M.C. there was a law, in Kipling's sense, and it was to be obeyed. A G.C. found pilfering small things from another cadet's pocket was tarred and feathered, horse-whipped across four hundred yards of lawn, and thrown into the freezing lake. He left . . . The crimes punished were lying to brother cadets, stealing from brother cadets, and in my case (I think), seeking the limelight. The R.M.C.'s ideas of punishment may have been barbaric, but the cadets had an unerring sense of crime . . . Inside the limits set by the code — and they gave a reasonable man plenty of room — it was an amazingly free life. . . .

Cheating was recognized as a form of work and had its own customs. It was permissible, indeed almost laudable, to cheat if that was your only hope of passing out and getting your commission. What did book learning matter, anyway, to a subaltern of a fighting regiment? It was not permissible to cheat in the hope of improving an already secure position, and most especially not in order to get a reward . . . It was my duty, at an examination, to put my worked papers in such a position that a desperate neighbour could look at them if he needed to cheat to avoid dropping a term. Whether he did look or not was his business. And if he was stupid enough to get caught, that was his business too. Damn it, a chap had to be good at something!'[7]

---

[7]*Bugles and a Tiger: a personal adventure* (Michael Joseph, 1956), Chapter 2. Masters has sometimes been criticized for presenting information on things which he did not experience at first hand. Nevertheless, his account is useful and informative.

THE TWENTIETH CENTURY:1900-35

# THE WAR YEARS: 1939–45

IN 1934 as the storm clouds gathered once again in Europe fourteen-day Territorial Army officer courses had been started at Sandhurst. But the officer-shortage problem remained acute up to the outbreak of war. (In 1937 the Willingdon Committee, investigating this, made the suggestion that the Army should seek its officers from grammar-school boys as well as those from public schools.)

In 1933 the Duff-Cooper Committee (chaired by Alfred Duff-Cooper, then Minister for Finance at the War Office) had suggested the amalgamation of Woolwich with Sandhurst as an economy measure, but after a violent protest from the Army Council the scheme was dropped. But amalgamation was again recommended by the Macdougall Committee in 1938, with the same core syllabus for all, and extra mathematics for the Artillery. This was accepted in June 1939, and would have come into force in August 1940 had war not broken out. Instead in September 1939 Woolwich simply closed down altogether and Sandhurst became OCTU (Officer Cadet Training Unit) Sandhurst, running sixteen-week courses throughout the War for infantry officers and a sixteen-week course with an extra eight weeks of special tactics and gunnery instruction at Bovington for those destined to become tank commanders. (As well as the Sandhurst OCTU, others opened up across the country and abroad.) Colonel Alan Shepperd, formerly chief librarian at Sandhurst and himself seriously wounded during the War, has written of those very active years:

'Sandhurst . . . was kept full to overflowing throughout the war. In January 1939 there were just over 600 gentleman cadets under training. By early July all but the junior term had been commissioned. The summer break was devoted to two courses for a total of 700 junior officers of the Territorial Army, and the new term opened with an intake of 271 gentleman cadets. Then, after a further six weeks, the previous juniors were passed out. Meanwhile, on mobilisation taking place, 550 officers and men of GHQ British Expeditionary Force assembled at the RMC prior to departure overseas. There was very tight security: Government House became a staging post for the Commander-in-Chief and some of his staff, and it was here that the Commander-in-Chief, Lord Gort, and HRH The Duke of Gloucester stayed on the night before they left for France.

On 4 September, the day after the war was declared, the RMC became the Sandhurst OCTU. There were two wings, the 101 Royal Armoured Corps Wing and the 161 Infantry Wing. The Inns of Court Regiment arrived as a complete unit, to start up the RAC Wing, while the RMC infantry cadets formed the nucleus of the Infantry Wing

**Opposite:**
Cadets at a Northern Command OCTU take the water jump during their 'Battle Training' (*Imperial War Museum*).

Physical Training on Assault Course, OCTU Sandhurst 1943 (*Imperial War Museum*).

under some of the existing staff. Cadets for the Cavalry, machine-gun units or corps were dispersed to OCTUs elsewhere.'[1]

Although the initial batch of wartime cadets came in the main direct from school or university, it was the practice throughout the War that all cadets should serve in the ranks before commencing their officer-training. Even though Sandhurst became, as it had in the first war, something of a sausage factory for officers, the prestige of its course was unaffected. All candidates to become officers in the Brigade of Guards automatically went there, rather than to any of the other OCTUs which had been set up. A member of my own family en route to the Irish Guards, who was at a Sandhurst OCTU early in the War, told me: 'We all had a common purpose that made it easier; it was all so rushed I don't remember much.' One notable feature of Sandhurst life during those hectic years was the presence of two companies of

[1] *Sandhurst*, p. 73.

**Opposite:**

The Riding School converted for instruction on tank mechanics for Royal Armoured Corps Cadets, OCTU Sandhurst 1943. (*Imperial War Museum*).

The Queen, accompanied by Princesses Elizabeth and Margaret, addresses a parade in Old College Square in 1941 (*Imperial War Museum*).

ATS. Although some old soldiers raised their eyebrows, the male officer cadets did not share their concern. More than a few smuggled themselves into the ATS lines for a bit of unofficial rest and recreation: '2 bottles of beer inside the battledress top' was the recognized pass! It would be thirty years before young women in uniform would be allowed back again in any significant number.

On a far sadder note, Sandhurst itself was bombed at least twice during the War. On the first occasion five cadets were killed in their rooms. There were no casualties on the next occasion. The second war, like the first, took a terrible toll, not only of the wartime cadets but of those young men who had studied there in earlier years. David Niven noted of his own Sandhurst peers, those who had been at the RMC in the late twenties:

'A heartbreakingly high percentage were destined . . . to meet death on the beaches, deserts and hillsides of World War II. For this was the vintage of soldiers that suffered most heavily when the holocaust came.'[2]

[2] *The Moon's a Balloon*, p. 63.

**Opposite:**
Confidence training at Southend for Officer Cadets attending an Eastern Command OCTU (*Imperial War Museum*).

# THE 'NEW' SANDHURST

The newly constituted Royal Military Academy Sandhurst opened in 1947. To watch over the birth there was a commandant with the rank of Major-General. Woolwich (or 'The Shop', as it had been known to generations of cadets) was gone for ever. The new title of Sandhurst Officer Training Establishment was a gesture to its old foe in so many rugby and cricket matches, but the reforms went deeper than the new name. In the 1945 election Attlee's Labour Party had achieved a surprise victory over Churchill's Tories. There was a mood of change in the country. The pre-war social order was no longer always taken for granted. In keeping with this trend, the young men arriving at Sandhurst would no longer be referred to as 'Gentlemen Cadets' but as Officer Cadets: they would all have served a term in the ranks, they would be paid, and (officially, at least) subject to military discipline, unlike their forebears at the RMC. A recruiting pamphlet produced in the late forties about Sandhurst attempts to convince possibly sceptical readers just how progressive Sandhurst had become:

'Throughout the daily routine of instruction and recreation, the 'new' Sandhurst aims at a blend of the traditional and the modern, the established and the experimental. It is a tentative mixture of laboratory and library, parade ground and playing field, university and technical college. It is organized on the basis of the spirit of the King's Commission, the tradition of service, the lessons of the recent war, and the necessity of making the Army Officer of today a trained citizen. . . .

It educates him in world affairs, scientific subjects, languages (including his too often neglected mother tongue) . . . It launches him on the first stage of a career for which he is specifically, not haphazardly, vaguely or accidentally trained. All is at the expense of the State.

This planned career is in no sense a class privilege. All Officer Cadets have to pass through the ranks before entry, and, subject to passing examinations and interviews, young men are accepted from all schools. In this way the Officer Cadet mixes with all classes of society, both in the months before entry and during his time at Sandhurst. In

Officer cadet J.A. Garnett, June 1947. (*Popperfoto*). The contemporary caption read 'The new Sandhurst: New type officers for a new style army are being created at Sandhurst where today's methods are being grafted on to yesterday's tradition.'

**Overleaf:**
Regimental J.C. Lord, MBE drills a squad, 1947. (*Popperfoto*).

addition, the British Commonwealth of Nations and many foreign countries send a quota of their future Officers to be trained at the Academy. The Officer Cadet thus rubs shoulders with people from all quarters of the globe, which is an education in itself. The experience of an education at Sandhurst, therefore, fits the future Officer for the modern British Army and the modern world. There is a close connection between good citizenship and good soldiering. The modern British Army by its very nature must be alert and alive to changing conditions. The education of its future Officers provides for this necessity.'[1]

**The pamphlet found it necessary specifically to counter criticism of the traditional Army and its officers which was prevalent at the time:**

'He (the Sandhurst student) is taught to consider past records and achievements neither as a fetish, nor as something discreditable . . . It has long been fashionable to mock the 'typical' Army Officer. Doubtless much of this mockery is based on familiarity. The largest proportion of men engaged in National Service in the last two great wars were in the Army. This universal aspect of the British Army means that it is criticized with the same frequency as one's home and one's family. Most of the criticisms are no longer relevant. Many discomforts will be rectified in the future, together with the discomforts of life in Great Britain generally, and at the same speed. The Officer Cadet at the Royal Military Academy Sandhurst will not in every case be a Sir Philip Sidney; but his parents and his teachers will have no cause to fear that his mind will be atrophied by the alleged narrowness of a supposedly intelligent career, or his development cramped by the typical comedy Sergeant Major.'[1]

**Perhaps the key point of the new Sandhurst, at least as it was planned, was the fact that civilian and military studies would carry almost equal weight; if anything the balance would be tipped in favour of the academic.**

'The Officer Cadet at the Royal Military Academy Sandhurst, after being commissioned, will . . . come into contact with the young men of Great Britain serving in the Army under National Service. His education is therefore of more than purely military importance. He will influence in some way, however slight, the lives of a score or more young citizens of Great Britain . . . Sandhurst enables the Officer Cadet to learn about the needs of humanity and of his own country, about the United Nations Charter and about important White Papers. . . .Some might criticise the curriculum as not being technical enough, in the sense that it is not entirely devoted to military and kindred subjects. A balance, however, has been struck between the professional requirements of an Officer's career and the requirements of a general education and citizenship. . .'[1]

**The new Sandhurst was designed to be almost a university or Academy in the truest sense; Le Marchant would have approved, his brain child had been allowed to atrophy and was at last being**

[1] *The Royal Military Academy Sandhurst* (RMAS, 1949).

**Left:**
The Library 1947.
(*Popperfoto*)

**Right:**
A tough time in the Hospital,
1947 (*Popperfoto*).

**Below:**
Officer Cadet Holloway
(foreground, and friends in
the FGS (Fancy Goods Store
— now the NAAFI) in 1947.

Officer Cadet King Hussein of Jordan at Sandhurst during 1952. (*Imperial War Museum; Sandhurst Collection*).

revitalized. To confirm its commitment to the modern, scientific citizen-soldier approach a civilian was appointed as the new 'Director of Studies'. His 'campus' was split into two faculties, one involved in teaching science and mathematics, the other, modern subjects and languages (French, German and, for the first time, Russian). On the military side there were four 'Wings' — drill and weapons training, driving and maintenance, fitness training and hygiene, and signal communications. Age on entrance was to be eighteen. The basic method of entry was through an examination set by the Civil Service Commission, from which exemption could be claimed on production of recognized qualifications (later five GCE passes, at least two at A Level). Five vacancies a year were held for cadets coming from the ranks, and another means of admission was via Welbeck College.

The basic pattern of Sandhurst courses remained the same until 1955, when the duration was increased from eighteen months to two years, to allow even more time for academic work. There would be one term of 'basic training' and five of 'professional studies'. As Sandhurst itself attempted to become more of a university, the Army, prompted by the Whistler Committee of 1958, became alerted to the need for more graduate officers. Having accepted that graduates were in principle a good thing, the Army faced (and indeed still faces) two alternatives: recruit graduates from civilian universities or produce their own 'in house'. Although the latter system is attractive in many ways — particularly for those young men entering technical arms — it is, of course, more expensive. The graduates that were entering the Army during the late forties and fifties were usually directly commissioned into a regiment after nominal service in their University Officer Training Corps. Few bothered to attend Sandhurst, although in principle they could if they were young enough.

In 1957 it was announced that National Service would end in three years, and in 1961 the Eaton Hall Office Cadet Training Unit at Chester was closed. This left the Mons OCTU, which had been the Royal Signals Officer Cadet Training Unit during the War, as the only institution training officers for short-service commissions.[2] The Mons course, later a great influence on Sandhurst, was of five months' duration. As short-service officers could extend the contract of their service after two or three years to become Regulars, Mons was often seen as something of a back door to a regular commission without the hard work of Sandhurst. Colonel Kenneth Timbrell, M.C., who used to be a senior instructor at Mons, told me what he considered the advantages of the Mons system were:

---

[2] Short Service Commissions had been introduced with National Service after the War.

**Left:**
Brushing up on the new technology, 1961. (*Imperial War Museum*).

**Right:**
The Library, 1961. (*The Photo Source*).

**Below:**
Finishing touches, 1961. (*The Photo Source*).

'At Mons we gave cadets a great deal of freedom. The course didn't attempt to bash everyone into the same mould, and I was told by commanding officers that they preferred the Mons man, who they found more mature. We mixed graduates and non-graduates, and found that this had a very positive effect.'

Throughout the 1960s, and in the midst of a general optimism about higher education, the trend to civilianize Army education which had begun after the War progressed. It did so despite widespread defence cuts. As the Empire vanished and the Army spent more of its time in barracks, it was assumed that officers would have careers and educational requirements little different from those of their civilian counterparts. In 1966 Michael Howard (now Regius Professor of Modern History at Oxford) and Cyril English produced an unofficial study on officer-education which, greatly influenced by the Robbins Report of 1963, called for a still wider general education. They wanted Sandhurst courses reduced to one year, but to be followed after two or three years service with the unit by a further year at a new Joint Services Defence Academy.

Edward Bear, Sandhurst's much travelled and decorated parachuting mascot.

West Point cadets visit RMAS in the 1960s (*Sandhurst Collection*).

By 1966 GCE examinations and the whole education structure which went with them had become well enough established for Sandhurst to drop its own entrance examination and depend entirely on this 'civilian' qualification for entrance. In 1969, at Howard's prompting, a civilian Advisory Council on officer-education was created, reporting to the Army board. It was made up of university dons and school headmasters. This resulted a year later in the 'academic year' concept at Sandhurst. Of the six terms available in the two-year course, the first one and the last two were to be given over to military matters under Army staff control, and the central 'year' of three terms left for solid academic work under the civilian staff. This had the advantage that students could give their best effort to academic studies unimpeded by any conflict with intensely physical military training. In other words, in theory at least, they had no excuse for falling asleep during lectures! The hope was to prepare cadets so that after eighteen months with their units they might go on to university, and the Advisory Council tried to institute a diploma for

A Burma Company ritual in the early 1960s (*Sandhurst Collection*).

the Sandhurst course which would count in part towards degree status. Their absolute ideal, endorsed on several occasions by Prince Philip among others, was for a university course in 'Military Science' at degree level as an accepted professional qualification.

All this was suddenly knocked away following the February 1971 Army review, which revealed a potential shortfall of 50 per cent in officer recruitment, with a further decline expected in the future. A working party was created by the Director of Army Training under Brigadier Tillard, and with considerable haste the Tillard Committee reported in November. A cynic might have predicted the result. It recommended a complete reversal of the civilian Advisory Council's principles. Mons, where officers for the increasingly popular Short Service Commissions had been trained since the War, would have to close as an economy measure. In future all officer-cadet training would take place at Sandhurst, but along accelerated Mons OCTU lines, and despite the fact that the original premise of such training, and of Short Service Commissions themselves, had been that young men were likely to have had experience in the ranks first. For the Regulars training would be substantially cut, particularly in the academic field. The main course at Sandhurst was to be the Standard Military Course of two terms totalling 25 weeks and covering basic Army skills. This would be completed by young men opting for both Short Service and Regular commissions. For those who had decided on a Regular Army career this would be followed, without a break, by the RCC (Regular Careers Course), a package of purely academic subjects lasting 21 weeks and later to be reduced even further. The subjects to be taught were to be war studies and international affairs; contemporary Britain; communications and comprehensions; and military technology. All language and mathematics teaching was to stop.

The Advisory Council was given a month before Christmas 1971 in which to comment on this. Despite its protests, and those of Sandhurst itself, the Army Board started to implement Tillard in March 1972. It prompted a fierce reaction from some of the Sandhurst civilian staff. The former Director of Studies, Geoffrey Sale, wrote to *The Times* to express an opinion shared by many:

'That a professionally trained officer can be produced able to cope with all situations and to understand the why and wherefore of his profession in 12 or 13 months is plainly ridiculous. It is to condemn the long-term officer who is not a graduate to being semi-educated, a worthy object of the B.B.C.'s caricatures.'

Recently there have been even more cuts to the academic side of Sandhurst which are discussed in detail in the next chapter. Academic

**Opposite:**
Sovereign's Parade, July 1965. (*Press Association*).

instruction since Tillard was strictly related to professional studies. Norman Dixon, the psychologist, has gone so far as to suggest that the military sometimes promotes anti-intellectualism, particularly in time of peace. When cuts have to be made, the Army will, if it has the choice, make them in the civilian preserves. (It is my own observation that the relationship between civilian and military staff at the RMAS remains a bit tense. Things were no doubt easier in the days after the War, when many academics had experience of military service. The military can be rather condescending towards their academic colleagues, although I doubt if they realize it. The academics, on the other hand, often appear to be slightly unsure of themselves. A fundamental problem is lack of effective communication between the two groups. One only has to witness the physical divide at morning coffee in the Officers' Mess between 'civvies' and 'soldiers' to appreciate this.)

The indecision and argument over the Sandhurst syllabus makes one thing plain: No one seems quite certain exactly what Sandhurst should be trying to achieve. Should it be an officer-cadet training unit with the emphasis on technical instruction, or should it be a true academy where a liberal education and advanced professional skills may be

Idi Amin (who did *not* attend Sandhurst) pays a visit in the early 1970s (*Sandhurst Collection*).

acquired? Whatever it may or may not be trying to achieve, one thing Sandhurst always remains is an initiation ceremony, a very visible process of socialization into the Officer Corps of the British Army. As far as this aspect of Sandhurst is concerned, perpetual tinkering with the course length and structure is not that important — now, if someone wanted to pull down the pillars of Old College that would be another matter!

I was first a student at Sandhurst in 1974, having previously completed a 'Brigade Squad', the potential Officer pre-RCB and pre-Sandhurst course of the Household Division. Sandhurst was for me, as it had been for so many before, a frantic experience. Drill, bull and more drill, endless digging in on barren Army Training Areas, getting lost while learning to map-read, and my own pet horror, PT. Because of the shortage of time, and despite herculean efforts by instructing staff, our professional skills did not seem to improve much, with the single exception of drill. Even though the Army was an unfashionable career at the time, we felt absolutely 'it', and sometimes behaved in an outrageously swaggering manner. Added to the effect of the official conditioning process was that resulting from our own social intercourse. Those who didn't 'know' picked up hints on how they should dress and act to fit in on- and off-duty. Such things were rarely discussed officially by instructors, who, incidentally, we came to love and hate in equal measure. There was a little bullying, far too much drinking and many pranks. A high point was the day someone glued a complete water-closet system on to the middle of Old College Square, and workmen were sent out the next morning to hack off the offending object before an imminent royal visit. Sandhurst was not enjoyable, it was very hard work. We felt we were being changed, and most wanted to be. There was some snobbishness, although it usually took relatively subtle form. Those destined for the Guards and Cavalry tended to stick together, and those who weren't going to 'smart' regiments (and I am not suggesting that only the Guards and cavalry regiments might be described as such), I think, resented this. Apart from a vague impression that it used to be even harder in the 'good old days' before the Second World War, we assumed Sandhurst was essentially an unchangeable and splendid monolith. We had absolutely no idea of the principles behind the post-war changes or of the behind-the-scenes wrangling over course content and duration. We did not see Sandhurst as a place where we learned to be soldiers; that would come later in our regiments. Sandhurst was where we learned how to get drunk like an officer and how to pick up girls from Winkfield. We would have been indifferent to any changes that might have been made to the professional aspects of the course. We quickly forgot most things force-fed into us, but would never forget the drill square and our friends.

To return to the more prosaic: in September 1973 both the military and civilian academy staff had reported that the Tillard scheme was not working well. The main problem was that the course was trying to do too much too quickly, and cadets were getting very stale. This led to a more formal enquiry in March 1973, the Committee on Army Regular Officer Training (CAROT). This, however, only rubber-stamped Tillard, being made up chiefly from the Director of Army Training's staff. The Academy was to try to attract more graduates. There was a parallel move to cut down the academic content of RCC, in which officers of the Army's own Education Corps were gradually to replace the civilian teaching staff (they have never been able to do so, to date). The Advisory Council opposed CAROT every step of the way, and in 1974 it was disbanded, or at least ceased to meet, as a result. The same year saw a reorganization of the civilian teaching staff to reflect Tillard. There were now three departments: war studies and international affairs; politics and social studies, with communications as a sub-branch; and military technology. The Soviet Studies Centre, staffed initially by former Sandhurst lecturers, was created at about this time. It has virtually no formal teaching role, and serves as a think-tank for observers of the Soviet armed forces.

In 1979 the RCC was reduced to one term of fourteen weeks and a gap of three or four years' service with unit introduced between SMC and RCC (some RCC candidates had always been 'returning officers' of the rank of captain who had decided to extend their commissions). CAROT had also introduced the 'PQS' (Promotion Qualification Standard) system of promotion examinations. PQS1 was the lieutenant-to-captain examination and PQS2 the captain-to-major examination, both completely independent of Sandhurst (except that some Sandhurst staff mark the papers). Increasingly, officers used RCC as a dry run to prepare for PQS2, and consequently more than one wary young captain was convinced that returning to Sandhurst might not be such a bad idea after all.

In 1977, in response to the continued short-fall in officer recruiting, a new and rather unusual twelve-week course was introduced at Sandhurst, Rowallan Company. It was designed along the lines of a similar course during the War, which had been used to boost the confidence of young men who in other respects were considered by a War Office Selection Board to be suitable applicants for a commission and might otherwise be rejected for officer training. Today's course is offered to some candidates by the Regular Commissions Board instead of an outright fail. Scouting by another name was how Lord Rowallan described the wartime course, and much the same can still be said of Rowallan, albeit very tough scouting indeed. Members of 'RowCo' all have to complete a journal; the extracts below are, believe it or not, fairly typical:

'*12th of January*: The driver who lifted our kit to the lines said to me, 'Rowallan company produces the best officers in the British Army, everyone knows that!' I remembered this, and no longer felt like a second-class citizen.

*14th of January*: Unfortunately I found out my level of fitness.

*15th of January*: It's difficult convincing yourself that you're getting better when you're constantly accused of slacking or ineptitude.

*17th of January*: Virtually everyone is broken now, we could be told to jump off a cliff and we would.

*22nd of January*: 4 o'clock rise in order to double back to camp from the field for an inspection at 6 o'clock. On to a slightly shorter endurance run than before, nevertheless involving various 1 in 2 hills, then endurance swimming of 12 lengths, one after another, then drill.

*28th of January*: I arrived at Hankley Common at about 3.30 a.m. and we had an 8 o'clock inspection. My feet were exhausted, flat and jaded. Since my stag [guard] was 4.30 to 5.30 I just stayed up and didn't bother going back to bed. It was so cold that my boots and my spare clothing inside my Bergan [rucksack] froze, but I was too tired to notice. My webbing fell apart at inspection.

*2nd of February*: I feel better now, I had a brief chat with the platoon commander and CSM, and have got my aims and attitudes sorted out. The things worth having have to be worked for.

*8th of February*: Today I saw a good doctor. He gave me some anti-vomiting syrup and liquid food.

*11th of February*: Well, here I am in hospital. My ankle isn't broken, it's only swollen up.

*17th of February*: I got 2 hours of sleep last night.

*18th of February*: My confidence in tackling any problem has increased massively. Nothing really awes me now and it feels so natural to be in command.

*23rd of February*: It was trog [yomping!] uphill and it was good to reach the snow line.

*24th of February*: My floor space did not pass inspection today, so tonight scrubbing and repolishing is in order. The good thing about the course is that it's demanding enough to take your mind off everything else.

*13th of March*: Today was spent recovering from Brecon Brenda [an exercise on the Brecon Beacon].

*24th of March*: A good time was had by all.'

Lord Rowallan's idea was to 'develop character first and military leadership will follow'. Rowallan is a physically demanding course but still achieves a pass-out rate of about 80 per cent.[3] The course has its critics, and rumours about it abound. The 20 per cent who fail the course are divided between those who are discharged for failing to

**Overleaf:**
Romanian officers on a four-day exchange visit, March 1978 (*Keystone*).

[3] The pass rate has increased in 1987; before it had been about 60 per cent and subject to criticism for that reason.

come up to the required standard, elect to leave prematurely, or are discharged on medical grounds. It is tough on the boys who don't make the grade; however, in spite of this and in spite of the slightly horrific picture painted by the cadet above, those who pass Rowallan are effusive in its praise.

Throughout the seventies and eighties, the Army began to attract more graduates, although the notional ideal of an all-graduate officer corps was still a long way off. CAROT had allowed Sandhurst to keep Pre-University Studies, a short course of about four weeks in which students who hoped to get into university on a cadetship were coached in technique and ways of passing A Levels. (PUS was finally abolished in 1985.) It was still normal during the seventies for university graduates to go straight to their units after service with the University Officer Training Course and a short supplementary officer course. A few — no more than forty a year — however, elected to come to Sandhurst for the DE, or Direct Entry, course, designed for graduates with no previous military experience. A similar number usually decided to join the Army while still at university, and did the slightly shorter POSUC (Post-University Cadets Course). In 1982, along with the other changes, DE and POSUC merged into the Standard Graduate Course of SGC. SGC, like the SMC, was two terms now of fourteen weeks each. Sandhurst admits that there have been a number of problems with its graduate courses. It sometimes seems, though, that the Army misunderstands graduates and the wide range of their abilities. One told me: 'The Army's concept of a graduate is of an Oxford First in PPE, whereas many of us have Thirds in Archaeology from Loughborough.' I completed a graduate course in 1980, just before the changeover to SPC. It was much easier in most respects than the SMC I had been on six years before. A friend, now a regular officer, who completed the same course commented:

'When I was at the RMAS in 1980 there was the feeling that graduates were there under sufferance and were not part of mainstream Sandhurst, a feeling underlined by the fact that we lived in rather grotty Victory College and 'passed off' its car park as opposed to Old College Square. We sometimes felt we were perceived as poets and basket weavers. We were always expecting the course to get tougher, but truthfully it never really did, although it was nevertheless hard, particularly in the psychological sense. It was also a little disappointing in that respect; also, several people passed in the course who we all felt frankly should not have been in the Army at all and who were quite unfit for command. They may have had degrees but this was not guarantee of their competence or leadership ability. If more people failed [more do now] we would have felt the course more worth-while. I suspect few did because the contemporary Army

policy was to raise the number of graduates in the Officer Corps. I found the academic content of the course rather superficial but it was a nice change from drill. From a professional point of view I think a lot of the drill and B.S. could be replaced by wider instruction in minor unit tactics, unit administration and weapons training. As an example there's no need to teach Officer Cadets rifle drill at all; they require only basic foot drill and sword drill. The time saved could be used to teach more useful professional skills. The argument that there must be rifle drill for the Sovereign's Parade doesn't hold water. In an age of cuts and searching for efficiency one must accept some reform of established ritual. Despite my criticisms, I am very proud of having passed through Sandhurst and will never forget the experience.'

The Graduate Course has changed considerably since my friend and I completed DE16. The SGC of today is twenty-eight weeks in duration, and students at the end of it now pass off on Old College Square with the SMC and WRAC. When graduate students leave Sandhurst they must now remain second lieutenants for a year; we were officially full lieutenants when we left, although many regiments insisted that the newly arrived graduates only wear one star, in keeping with their 'still wet behind the ears' status. To arrive displaying full lieutenant's rank could put some people's noses out of joint, and also made it difficult for the new officer to make mistakes in front of other ranks. (Graduate students at the RMAS wear a single star from their first day, but at the

The Spanish Defence Minister watches training in 1980. Sandhurst acts as host to a huge number of visiting VIPs every year (*Topham*).

moment it is being considered whether this practice should be continued. It is thought that the privilege of allowing probationary officers to wear such obvious rank may not be in keeping with the ethos of the Sandhurst Course. It is probable that they will soon wear a star on a lapel gorgette instead. The non-graduates already wear a button on a gorgette.) If a graduate fails to pass through the SGC for medical or other reasons now he may be put on to an available SMC with the younger non-graduates. When this does occur there appear to be few problems and it would tend to indicate that male graduates and non-graduates can indeed be taught together, as they were at Mons.

The remaining changes at the RMAS until last year (1986) and the Rote report, have not been great, with one very significant exception: the arrival of the women. In 1981 the Officer Cadets and graduate Probationary Officers of the WRAC College down the road in Camberley started being bussed to Sandhurst for lectures. In 1984 the WRAC College closed to become a 'Wing' in Sandhurst's own Old College. The course — in emulation of the old Mons course for young men — was taught to a mixture of graduates and non-graduates. Until September 1986 it was twenty-five weeks long, but this had the disadvantage that female students arrived at the RMAS some three weeks after their male counterparts. It is now twenty-eight weeks long, and the course taught is in many respects similar to SGC, with whom they share about 20 per cent of their training, mostly in the classroom and joint lectures. It is interesting to note that the female non-graduates seem to have no problem keeping up academically with their graduate companions, either male or female. The WRAC do fewer field exercises and less weapons training than the young men of SGC. Lieutenant-Colonel Susan Wing points out: 'We are not trying to turn out infantry platoon commanders.' Reflecting the posts most will take up, the course concentrates on clerical, administrative and teaching skills. Unlike other Sandhurst courses for men, it attempts to produce an immediately employable product. Many young women from the WRAC go on to jobs as assistant Adjutants soon after leaving Sandhurst. Socializing with the young men from New and Old Colleges, within the limits of Academy discipline, is not discouraged. Those limits are that male and female cadets will not visit each other's rooms, and that any female cadet who gets pregnant must leave.

By way of consolidation and before considering Sandhurst today in detail, it is useful to examine something of the organization which has developed over the preceding years. Sandhurst has three principal colleges, New, Old and Victory. New College is the home of the Standard Military Course, the basic course for non-graduate potential officers. Its NCO instructing staff, unlike those at other colleges, are recruited exclusively from the Brigade of Guards, Instructing Officers may come from anywhere in the British Army. Old College, the original Sandhurst College building, is, as we have noted, home to the WRAC Course, and also to the new Junior Command and Staff Course (of which more later), two-week TA Officer courses (both male and female) and the four-week CMVDLP Course (Chaplains, Medics, Vets, Dentists, Legal and Post, commonly known as 'Tarts and Vicars'!) The Old College commander, a colonel, like the commanders of New and Victory Colleges, is also responsible for Rowallan Company, although the latter has its own accommodation and offices.

Old College, by far the most majestic of the Sandhurst College buildings, is currently being renovated. In 1989 the graduates who at the moment occupy modernistic Victory College, Sandhurst's least prestigious building, will move to Old College — a significant step reflecting their increased status generally. The WRAC Course — to be renamed The Women's Standard Course (WSC) from September 1987 — and the others taking place at Old College will take the graduates' place at Victory.

Although they are restricted in some ways, colonel commanders of Sandhurst colleges have at the moment considerable freedom as far as such things as methods of assessment of students are concerned. However, with so many relatively senior officers in such a confined space it is perhaps inevitable that the occasional clash of interests occurs. It is the Commandant's task to keep these to a minimum, and to preserve the stability and efficient administration of the Academy in general. He is also in overall command of various administrative departments, the Gurkha Demonstration Company, and the several specialist training wings (Skill at Arms, Signals and PT). He works from Academy headquarters, a modern building in the same style as Victory College. The Assistant Commandant, the Adjutant, Academy Sergeant-Major (arguably the most senior NCO in the British Army) and Academy Press Officer also work from this bulding, as well as a number of secretarial and clerical personnel, and those officers involved in training development. Postings to Sandhurst for most officers last two years, although there is a possibility of extension.

The remaining courses currently being taught at Sandhurst and not yet mentioned are the one-week Cadet Force Officer course, the three-week Short Service Limited Commission course undertaken by students who wish to put off going to university to serve with a unit for $x$ months as a temporary officer, and the six-week NCO 'Cadre' course for incoming non-commissioned instructors. The pass rate of the latter is about 70 per cent, and after completing a tour at Sandhurst a senior sergeant can expect to rise quickly to the heights of the NCO rank structure.

# SANDHURST TODAY: THE ROTE REPORT

L EFT to its own devices the natural process of change at Sandhurst would in all probability not be a very rapid one. In this Sandhurst differs little from other long-established institutions, military or civilian. However, in recent years Sandhurst has not been left to its own devices; it has been, as we have noted, the subject of an inordinate number of committees and study groups. The latest of these, led by Major-General Jeremy Rougier, gave birth to 'The ROTE Report' (The Review of Officer Training and Education). ROTE's brief, as suggested by its full title, extended beyond Sandhurst but it is in its proposals for officer-training and education at the RMAS that it is controversial. The assumptions made by the authors make interesting reading:

'The trend will be for the size of the Army to decrease both because of the greater cost effectiveness of ET [Emerging Technology] systems and because of budgetary considerations . . . There will be an increasing requirement for all officers to be technically literate . . . It will be increasingly difficult to recruit officers of the desired standard into the army, as the pool from which they are drawn contracts. This pool (those with a minimum 2 'A' Levels) will decrease by some 20% in the next 10 years. . . The supply of science-based officers will continue to fall some way short of demand . . . about 55% of officers at the Captain level are likely, in the future, to have a degree (compared) with the present figure of 46% of all regular Captains and 26% of all officers in the Army). In the near future, the graduate officer will be the norm. . . First, potential officer recruits will continue to be drawn from the less traditional sources and from schools that tend to concentrate on academic achievement rather than character development and leadership. Secondly, potential officers will be better educated and will expect and accept a degree of intellectual challenge in their military career. Thirdly, officers will be less committed to the Army as a long term career, and will seek material rewards and more immediate job satisfaction if they are to remain. [ROTE report restricted]'

Considering such assumptions, the ROTE authors came to some surprising conclusions. Before examining the controversial points it is perhaps as well to consider one suggestion which has been almost universally accepted as sensible, the increase of the Standard Military Course — the basic course for male non-graduates — from two terms to three. The two-term course has for some time been considered far too short. Three terms allow more time to use the facilities at Sandhurst and for group spirit to develop, and the two vacations enable cadets to extend their adventure training.[1] It will also allow for some academic content, which was not previously a feature of the SMC.

Even with these changes, the main component of the SMC was, and will remain, basic military skills and drill. The MOD agreed to the substantial extension of SMC on condition that no further money would be forthcoming for the Sandhurst budget, and economies must be made accordingly. This, of course, was where ROTE was inevitably going to create ill feeling.

The male graduates coming to Sandhurst in the future will have the academic side of their course drastically reduced, even though the academic component previously taught concerned international affairs and war studies, subjects unfamiliar to the vast majority of them. One told me:

'I think it's a ridiculous decision. The academic side of the course was one of the few parts which we all enjoyed and thought was useful. Apart from anything else it keeps us sane and was a break from the B.S. of polishing boots. I covered subjects which I had little knowledge of before, and I'm sure it will contribute to my effectiveness as an Army officer, even though it might have done little to improve my performance as an infantry lance corporal on exercise.'

The official line is that the loss of the academic component to the Standard Graduate Course will be no great loss, as despite the opinion expressed above, it covered ground familiar to many and was fairly short anyway. There is some truth in this argument, but perhaps the real problem is that the academic component has to date not been long enough. The WRAC course — soon to be renamed the WSC (The Woman's Standard Course) — the extension of which from twenty-five to twenty-eight weeks was confirmed by ROTE, and which is modelled on SGC, also loses most of its academic component. Approximately sixty periods have been whittled down to eighteen, the extra time being used to teach additional tactics and administrative skills. The WRAC instructing staff are not at all pleased by this move,

---

[1] During the recess students must undertake some approved activity. Many opt to attend a UEL (Unit Expedition Leaders') course in Wales.

stating that it is a step in the wrong direction.

Another casualty of ROTE is the old Regular Careers course, which non-graduate officers used to do at Sandhurst after two to four years of service. There is a new and much shorter academic package, which has been added to the old professional skills JCSC (Junior Command and Staff Course). The new JCSC has a number of phases; as well as four weeks of academic work at Sandhurst consisting of international affairs, military history and war studies, students must complete a three-week military technology course at Shrivenham and, as always, a ten-week Warminster course. This includes basic staff work, tactics at company level, intelligence and service writing, and finally a correspondence course which is marked from Sandhurst. Without driving readers to distraction by quoting more Army initials, it is enough to note that, together with JCSC, there is a new set of promotional exams officially labelled JOTES (don't ask!).

The thinking behind JCSC appears to be that the average officer in the early years of his career does not need a general education. He can be taught more economically in blocks, preferably with his regiment rather than in a formal academic setting, with new courses being 'bolted on' as he progresses through the Army. Therefore, less formal academic instruction is required. Coupled with this is a growing desire for 'relevance', a belief that the officer should concentrate only on matters affecting the likely role of BAOR in the Central Front against Soviet opposition or internal security at home or in Ulster. All this is broadly in keeping with the provisions of the 1981 Defence Review, although it ignores the point that the main value of an education is teaching someone the habit and methods of being able to learn — vital skills for junior and senior commanders alike.

The axe has also fallen on some of the academic departments at Sandhurst; the remainder face privatization. Military technology is to go altogether, an extraordinary choice considering the increasing importance of its subject. Any Army scientific teaching in the future is to be undertaken by The Royal Military College of Science at Shrivenham, as with JCSC. In 1985 the War Studies and International Affairs department (WS&IA) was eighteen strong; it is now twelve strong. In addition, some departments are being reorganized. What was the Communications Section has been elevated to become the Communications Department, emphasizing the growing importance of the media and all related to it. The Department of Politics and Social Studies has taken the International Affairs component from WS&IA to become the Department of Defence Studies and International Affairs. WS&IA has become the Department of War Studies and Military History. This curious position of two departments apparently with very similar names has been widely interpreted (not least by War

Studies members) as a move to close their department down in a few years' time, and several are now looking for new jobs. The department has already lost its best-known member, John Keegan, in 1986 to the *Daily Telegraph*, where he has since gained a reputation as an outspoken defence correspondent.

Normal academic relations at the RMAS were overseen by a civilian Director of Studies and his deputy. They will continue to hold their posts. However, the changes are being overseen by a brigadier, leading to some speculation that the role of civilian Director of Studies may also go. Many of the academic staff are extremely bitter about both the changes and the manner in which they were carried out, although one must also note that the changes described are in some respects similar to those which took place within civilian higher education a decade ago.

The present changes closely follow the experience of the early 1970s. Just as CAROT rubber-stamped Tillard, so the ROTE report of 1985 has rubber-stamped the earlier Beach Report of 1984. In this case at least the Army had the sense to wait for the rubber stamp before implementing the changes. Again the motives for change, officer-shortage and the need for economy, are the same. But whereas after each major war this century the conclusion has been solidly with the 'wider' view, as in Akers-Douglas after the Boer War, Haldane after the First World War and the reconstituted RMA Sandhurst after the Second World War, the work of Tillard/CAROT Beach and ROTE marks the triumph of the 'Army' view. Some comments on ROTE from Sandhurst academic staff include:

'To overturn this would require either the effects of a major war, which seems excessive, or a general study of Army education conducted by politicians and civilians.

ROTE has been written and implemented in conditions of considerable secrecy. The team interviewed no members of the teaching staff at RMAS below departmental head, . . . while it was going on we were told we couldn't comment because it was *sub judice*. And when it was finished we couldn't comment because it was *fait accompli*.

It puts officer training in the British Army almost ludicrously out of step with that of every other Army of a major power, all of which run courses of between two and four years in length. In an age when being a soldier is becoming ever more complicated this is an extraordinary decision.

Its basic philosophy, that additional modules of education can be bolted on at various points of an officer's career, is supported by no known educational theory, it ignores the fundamental point that what education teaches is the skills and habits of how to learn, and it invites narrow-mindedness on the part of those who are taught in this manner.

The changes taking place at the RMAS are therefore committed to a philosophy that serving officers do not require any form of academic education, and in particular none in the political and social sciences, nor do they need to make serious study of the history of warfare or of military thought outside the immediate role of BAOR in NATO. Or, at least, that if they do need to do so they may receive this education later in their careers, at the staff college.

There is no evidence at all to support the report's assumption that in future officers with degrees — who will still form only 55% of regular Captains — particularly science degrees, will have any previous knowledge of war studies, contemporary affairs or communications. Nor is there any evidence to support its assumption that officers, with degrees or without, from what it calls "less traditional sources", i.e. from other than public schools, will be lacking in leadership qualities.

The proposed changes will mean the end of 'education' as such, at RMAS. It will be replaced instead with 'instruction', in which the candidate will absorb by rote as it were so much communications theory, international relations or military history in much the same way as he would learn to field-strip a rifle.

The fundamental question is whether Sandhurst will truly remain the Royal Military Academy or whether it will end up as merely an officer cadet training unit.'

A lecturer in the doomed Military Technology Department made an unprecedented contribution to the *Wish Stream*, Sandhurst's in-house magazine in the autumn of 1985:

'From 1947 to 1972, the educational content of the Sandhurst course for Career Officers was approximately 45%. Among the many cogent reasons put forward for this large admixture of tertiary education was: the need to lay early firm foundations and habits of scholarship for a whole career which required a constant up-date of knowledge, the refining of sound judgement from a critical appreciation of all human, political, historical, economic and technical factors which affect military decision-making at the level eventually required. The seed of successful generalship had to be sown early, it was felt . . .

In 1972, following the co-location with MONS Officer-Cadets' college, in an endeavour to improve recruiting, the educational Regular Career Course was cut to one term, following commissioning after two military terms. Alone in NATO, we were able to produce a non-graduate 2Lt in eleven months, including 5 weeks' leave. . .

The report purports to propose a welcome increase of SMC by one term. This increase, however, would be paid for by concentrating the educational content of RCC into four weeks' work in two academic Departments at Sandhurst, whilst Military Technology would be reduced to a high-density, competitively priced, three-week course at Shrivenham.

Is such criticism justified? It certainly cannot be denied that ROTE is a cost-cutting exercise, as this is made quite clear in the committee's terms of reference:

'The aim of this study is 'to define the essential common training, including education, required by regular officers during their careers and to recommend a programme for that training which is balanced, progressive and cost effective'. We were given 2 overriding priorities:

**a.** To ensure than no officer spends longer on courses than is necessary to prepare him for his role.

**b.** Whilst maintaining the high quality of training, to carry out such training as economically and efficiently as possible.'

The pro-ROTE argument is that limited resources must now be concentrated on individuals only when it is clear that they wish to make a career in the Army. The Army has been worried that it has been wasting valuable resources on the growing number of Short Service Commission officers who have elected to leave the service after only a few years. The concern is understandable, but there is a danger in this line of argument, as it tends inevitably, by way of justification, to devalue the broad benefits of a liberal education.

The arguing over ROTE is actually symptomatic of a much deeper clash of philosophies. Cathy Downes, a research Fellow in the Department of Political Science at the University of Melbourne, has written about the problems surrounding the reconciliation of a liberal education experience with vocationally relevant training:

'Almost invariably, each activity inhibits, undermines and impinges upon the needs of the other. The philosophy which supports academic education emphasises reflection, reading, reasoning and the presentation of ideas and thoughts in both written and verbal mediums. Activity centres on the individual and the maturation and expansion of his thought processes. A diverse range of subjects may be studied which need have little functional relevance to the final employment pursuit taken up by the student.

In contrast, the philosophy which supports training tends to be functional, vocational and job-specific. Particularly in the military context, training tends to be group-oriented and directed towards the individual subsuming his personal identity, needs and wants beneath the identity and needs of the group. The emphasis is upon team-work and immediate coordinated obedience to externally-imposed directives. Military training, with its emphasis upon conformity, constraint and order is designed to ensure that 'fear is stilled, aggression evoked and disorder prevented'. However, these goals are achieved at a price. Conformity, constraint and order are total concepts. The achievement of these desired states requires the suppression, eradication or removal of the disorderly, the non-conformist and the unrestrained.'[2]

As an academic she states an opinion which many of her colleagues at Sandhurst might share:

The goals and activities of a liberal education are perceived to be in almost complete opposition to those of vocationally relevant training. Most in military organisations have come to accept that raw courage, ritual and regulations, while having a part to play, cannot alone guarantee success on the battlefield, whatever its character. However, while accepting the need for officers to engage in activities which open and stretch their minds, the military organisation has sought to impose its own sense of orderliness upon the administration and operation of educational activities. Thus, it would seem fair to observe that the idea of a liberal education in a military training establishment is a flawed one. Experience to date has proven that the commitment of military authorities to education is often restrained and qualified. For their part, most academic professionals are sceptical of the sincerity of the military's commitment to an environment of free expression and existence; both of which are considered vital preconditions of an eduacational environment. The lack of tolerance, understanding and middle ground often leads to a battle. A conflict which involves tactics of over-loaded curricula. carrot and stick assessment policies and power-politicking in policy committees. The irony is that the pawn, and very often the loser, in this battle is the officer cadet, the very person who both groups are ostensibly trying to help.[2]

The clash which Cathy Downes describes is clear at Sandhurst today. The military party, to which it should be noted not all Army officers belong, is the temporary victor. In the future, though, the Army must be the poorer and probably less effective because of the dismembering of such an important part of Sandhurst. Even should the will exist in the future to rebuild it, much is being irretrievably lost — not least the goodwill of the staff. Even if it is expensive, there is no adequate justification for giving officers a narrower education in an ever more complex and dangerous environment.

The anti-ROTE lobby should not have the only word. The former Commandant, Major-General R.C. Keightley C.B., in writing a special foreword to the Spring 1986 edition of the *Wish Stream* to coincide with the implementation of ROTE gave his qualified approval:

'The need for these changes has been justified by use of the systems approach to training. After thorough consultation throughout the Army the job specification for a young officer leaving Sandhurst was produced. The training objectives of the commissioning courses needed to achieve that job specification were then worked out and new courses are now being designed to meet those. With one proviso the changes are very much what we at Sandhurst have long felt to be necessary.'

[2] *RUSI Journal*, Vol. 131, No 4 (Dec, 1986), pp. 13-24.

'The proviso is the loss of the Regular Careers Course; replacing that with two phases, totalling 7 weeks, of the Junior Command and Staff Course does have considerable advantages, but there is a possible drawback too. However, that possible drawback is going to be very carefully monitored. Under the new arrangement both graduate and non-graduate regulars will receive the same academic instruction, short-service graduates will not have to waste their limited time on the Standard Graduate Course absorbing academic knowledge they do not need and regular non-graduates will not have to return to Sandhurst just at the time when they are most needed as troop or platoon commanders by their commanding officers. But it is possible that non-graduate regulars will fall behind their graduate contemporaries intellectually during the very concentrated phase 1 of the JCSC and never subsequently catch up. However, if that happens it will be detected early and remedial measures taken.

One effect of these changes is going to to be the disbandment of the Military Technology Department. Financial necessity has forced the centralization of all military technology teaching to the Royal Military College of Science at Shrivenham. So another long established part of Sandhurst is having to go the same way as the Band Corps did two years ago. That is a sad loss. But I am glad that at least a computer facility is to remain in being and am most grateful to the other members of the Military Technology Department for their philosophical acceptance of the situation and their continuing support while there remains a job for them to do.

Overall, though, apart from the loss of the Military Technology Department, we can be well pleased with the planned changes. In the foreword I wrote in Spring 1984 I forecast that life could never stand still at the Academy. These latest changes are a continuation in the evolution pattern of courses that was first introduced in 1972. The changes will make our training better balanced, more effective and more enjoyable for the students. I am delighted all this is now being achieved.'

Keeping Sandhurst in tune with the needs of society and of the Army is without doubt a tough task. Constant monitoring is of course part of that task, and structures need to be developed which are adaptable. In a well-developed system it should be possible to introduce changes without disruption. One might even suggest that in Sandhurst's case there should now be some form of permanent study group to help achieve this. It does not seem to make sense, however, to constantly take one step forward and two backward. However, there is no such thing as perfection in human endeavours, and whatever system is adopted mistakes are inevitable. The situation is made even more difficult because Sandhurst's role has become confused as things around it change so quickly.

Sandhurst's prime stated aim remains to teach young men and women to be leaders in a military environment. However, the way in which that goal is achieved is changing because of a number of factors, not least the increasing cost of training, the Army's perception of the needs of the new technology and the changing social base of the officer corps (itself reflecting significant changes in the society as a whole). The Army may have little or no control over outside society, inflation or the growth of technology (even though the 'Defence market' is a massive customer of high-tech industries), but it tries to retain an iron grip over its own social structure regardless of the origins of those who enter it. One reason for the extension of the Standard Military Course is that it will allow more time for the military socialization of those students from what the Army describes as 'non-traditional' backgrounds. Integrating new technology and methods while trying to maintain a relatively static, somewhat contrived but familiar social structure is likely to be a tough task. How the young men and women of today, destined to become commanders in this slightly schizophrenic environment, should be prepared and/or educated is a question indeed.

# METHOD AND ASSESSMENT

The official aim of today's
course.

ALTHOUGH the precise function and aims behind it sometimes appear a little confused, the training which Officer Cadets and probationary officers receive at today's Sandhurst has a common pattern. Officially at least, it is all designed to promote leadership. It begins, however, with what David Niven called 'the mud treatment', five weeks of joy bulling kit, sweating and being sworn at on the drill square. This introduction has been a feature of Sandhurst life for generations, and whatever criticisms one might make, it is without doubt a most significant part of the Sandhurst tradition, and one which many would look back upon with a degree of affection. Major Malcolm Flower-Smith told me:

'It is a fairly hard period, but not nearly as hard as what the 'plebes' [freshmen] at West Point go through. There's a purpose, of course, to this hard five weeks. We're trying to build them into a team. We're trying to reduce individuality to some extent. We're not trying to make robots out of them. We're trying to reduce individuality in order to build an identification within them towards the Academy, towards the Army, towards their first Unit, which is their college, and towards their first sub-units, their company and their platoon. To do that, you have to change attitudes and changing attitudes is always difficult; what the psychologists call breaking down and building up. It's not really as vicious as brain-washing. It's a form of social engineering; it's uncomfortable but then there's a great deal of getting together. They get together to face discomfort and gather strength from each other. They're all going through it, they're all getting up at five o'clock and going on runs and spending hours and hours bulling their boots and cleaning their rooms until after midnight. It's misery for everybody but out of the misery they begin to identify as a group, and it's a short period of time.'

Even after students 'pass off the square' in the fifth week, drill remains a key element in their Sandhurst training, ending via the Sovereign's Platoon competition[1] at the end of the first term, with the fine

[1] As well as drill the competition includes a 'march and shoot', orienteering and a steeplechase.

pageantry of the Sovereign's Parade. Can one justify so much drill in what is already a short course? Drill may promote group cohesiveness, it just might make individuals react more swiftly to words of command in battle, but most of all it looks good. Sandhurst is about looking good, and especially looking good to outsiders at home and abroad. Although there are some differing views on the broader benefits of drill (some critics argue it would be more useful to develop group spirit via skills which were professionally relevant), it gives potential officers a taste of what their soldiers have gone through as recruits.

During the first weeks, slightly dazed and sleep-deprived students are also taught about the structure of the Army, its Regiments and Corps. They are rapidly introduced to map-reading, basic tactics, weapons handling, radio signalling and nuclear, biological and chemical warfare (NBC). The male graduates, unlike their fellow students on SMC, undertake a preliminary Exercise 'First Flush' in their second week, before 'passing off the square', in which basic field-craft skills are taught. Field Exercises are a fundamental part of all Sandhurst courses. Students receive, and are minutely assessed upon 'command appointments' during exercises corresponding to appointments within an infantry platoon. There are a fixed number of exercises for each course, and in the case of SMC and SGC the last major exercise is usually overseas, infantry exercises are a very significant part of Sandhurst training. To return to Major Flower-Smith:

'Our method is to use the vehicle of infantry tactics and specifically the infantry platoon, as it's a common beast to all arms, to give experience in command. If a young man is going to go to the RCT, or REME or the Royal Signals, he still needs infantry tactics because he may be called upon to defend his workshop, or relay station or whatever. Although our Charter is to give basic skills training, one should be quite clear, however, that primarily Sandhurst is here to develop leadership in young men and it is on their potential and their development of their potential for leadership that they are assessed and the decision is made as to whether they stay, whether they are back-squadded or whether they are kicked out. What we are not so interested in is if they can dig a bloody good slit trench. We are more interested in whether they can get others to dig slit trenches. The level of skills they build up for themselves is less important than their ability to command other people. They go on to their individual Arms Schools and do their young officer course after they leave Sandhurst and that is where they develop their real skills. It is often jokingly said that no one left Sandhurst for lack of military skills, but you will leave Sandhurst for lack of officer qualities.'

Although Sandhurst instructors will tell one making mistakes is an accepted and important part of a student's training, a bad mistake made by a student on exercise can be hard to atone for. The student who 'makes a pig's ear of it' — the dread of everyone being watched while in a command appointment — will let himself in for special scrutiny. While some no more talented individuals may slip through the Sandhurst net, the individual who has been seen to fail in command can be sure of another even more taxing command appointment in the next exercise. For some cadets the fear of failure can become a barrier to progress, and for a few it may lead to them being back-termed or asked to leave the Academy. The officer cadet or probationary who has some experience of basic tactics — as have many of those who have completed 'O type' potential officer courses in the ranks — finds himself with a major practical advantage, especially in the first term, although this tends to evaporate quickly thereafter.

Several of the students I interviewed told me about their analysis of

the Sandhurst system and the way they modified their behaviour to meet it. They talked of 'staying in the grey', the practice of not drawing the attention of the Instructing Staff to them. Their belief was that if one was not 'blade runner (sword of honour candidate)', then it was better to stay firmly in the background. Showing too much talent invited disaster; it was far too risky. One officer at Sandhurst, attached from another service, told me that he thought the current Sandhurst system, which rarely rewarded the taking of risks, could lead sometimes to the production of rather over-cautious inflexible young commanders.

Spend any time at all at Sandhurst and one will hear a great deal about leadership. Promoting leadership, in those already selected as

Preparing orders.

## LEADERSHIP PRACTICAL TASKS – FUNCTIONS CHECKSHEET

| PHASES | Achieve task (a) | Build/Maintain TEAM (b) | Develop/Satisfy INDIVIDUAL (c) |
|---|---|---|---|
| PLANNING | Define the task<br>Obtain Information<br>Make Appreciation<br>Make a plan | Involve Team in Planning<br>Detail Groups<br>Appoint Sub leaders | Assess the skills potential of each man<br>Use knowledge and Expertise of Individuals to assist in making your Plan |
| BRIEFING | State Aim<br>Issue Orders | Give clear orders<br>Expalin reason for Task<br>Set Standards/Priorities | Delegate<br>Check the Individuals understand the Plan |
| CONTROLLING | Ensure that all Activity is directed towards achieving the Aim<br>Monotor Progress<br>Re-plan if necessary | Coordinate<br>Maintain Standards | Maintain Standards |
| SUPPORTING | Provide Resources | Maintain Team Spirit | Encourage Individuals<br>Criticise constructively<br>Look after administration |
| INFORMING | Keep yourself informed of progress in all areas | Keep team in the picture on Progress<br>Ensure communication within the Team | Thank and Praise |
| EVALUATING | Review Tasking. Has Aim been Achieved? | Recognise Success<br>Learn from Failure | Listen to Feedback<br>Assess Performance |

having the potential, is of course a fundamental part of all officer-training. Sandhurst has adopted a theoretical model of leadership developed by one of its former lecturers, the psychologist John Adair. The adoption of Professor Adair's 'functional' approach has influenced many aspects of the syllabus. Attempts to promote leadership are made in a variety of practical contexts, but it is also taught as a specific classroom subject (over eighty periods for SMC and about sixty each to SGC and WRAC). Adair's theory suggests that the successful leadership of the group depends on the leader satisfying three sets of needs; those of the task, those of the group and those of the individual; and fulfilling six functions: planning, briefing, controlling, supporting, informing and evaluating (see diagram). As one member of the staff notes:

'It gives both students and directing staff a theoretical framework and a practical checklist, something to hang their hat on. If the student and instructor are both using the same list, assessment is made much easier.'

A critic of the Adair system as utilized at Sandhurst might say that what is being tested is the ability to apply the system rather than leadership itself. The possible danger exists that it might tend to produce a homogenized 'pattern-following' sort of leader if it is followed too slavishly as, by its nature, it does not appear to leave that much room for individuality of style. However, the majority of instructors do not follow the model slavishly; rather they use it as a starting-point. Nevertheless the widespread acceptance of the functional model does indicate a significant change in the Army's approach to man and systems management, and one which is paralleled by similar developments in industry and commerce. In an age of cuts and computers, such an easily demonstrable and definable system evidently has its attractions. Perhaps it is also significant that one can now buy camouflaged file-o-fax in the Camberley military surplus shop!

Another important part now of all Sandhurst courses which like the concern for 'scientific' management parallels similar developments in the corporate world is Communications Studies. The emphasis given to this type of training reflects the Army's concern with its public image and its desire to promote more effective communication among all ranks. In the context of Sandhurst it is also used to develop individual confidence and self-awareness.

Heather Duncan, Head of Sandhurst's Communications Department, reflected:

'We're relatively new, being in existence since October 1986. We grew out of the Communications section of the previous Department of Political and Social Studies. The fact that we have been formed in our own right shows the growing awareness of good communication, not just in the service environment but throughout industry. We are trying to keep as wide a base in human communication skills as possible whilst working within the limitations of a military environment and trying to relate and respond to military requirements. The type of oral communication we do, for example, reflects very closely the presentation of orders and briefings; although we also practise the other aspects, which perhaps have been overlooked in the past, such as the relationship between officers and soldiers in terms of counselling and general welfare. We feel this is reflecting changes in society as a whole. We are putting more emphasis on the new Standard Military Course, on extending the time that we give to such interviewing skills. On SMC, they will now have fifty-nine hours of communications training; before ROTE they had about twenty. The graduates will still only have about twenty hours, and the girls the same because they are taught alongside the male graduates. However, we find that graduates, although their written communication might be a little better, in effect still have the same communication needs and I think they could equally benefit from a longer course. . . . We work up from quite simple interviewing skills to learning how to respond to more aggressive, more probing questioning which students might receive at the scene of an incident. Obviously, in some arenas today they are protected more than

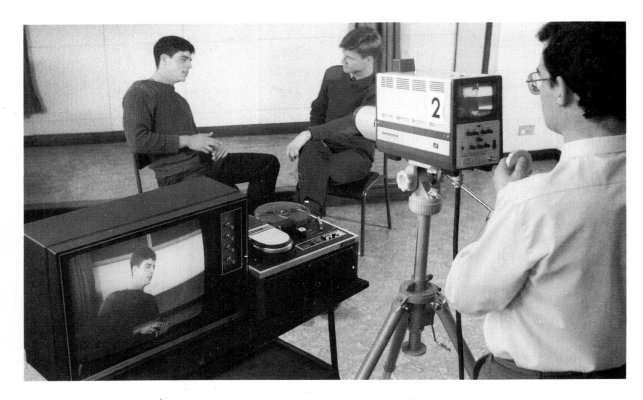

they were ten or fifteen years ago from this type of approach by the media. . . . Our students' learning curve is quite steep. Initially, they make quite dreadful mistakes which one hopes at the next opportunity, for real outside, they will not repeat. . . . We have responsibility for the television studio, the CCTV network within the Academy, and all the television work that goes on. We find the payback we get from that in terms of pure student learning is far and away ahead of the time we can give it; the average television exercise is 1½ hours, where effectively they perhaps have only 3½ minutes in front of the camera. It really is tremendous payback for us in terms of debriefing and their learning.'[2]

Practising interview technique in the CCTV studio (*Central Office of Information*).

There was a universal consensus among students that I spoke to that communications studies was useful and enjoyable.

One of the more unusual responsibilities of the Communications Department is to play a hostile television news crew during the major internal security exercise which both SGC and SMC undertake at the specialist urban warfare training area at Longmore.

Heather Duncan and her colleagues make a real film of the exercise and then cut it misrepresentatively to show how the media might project a false image. The introduction of a substantial internal

[2] Interview with author.

security (also known as CRW[3]) training into the Sandhurst syllabus reflects the Army's involvement in Ulster and the world-wide increase in terrorism. Students who receive considerable instruction in basic skills for coping with riots and patrolling urban areas at Sandhurst as well as on exercise are also made aware of their potential IS role, and its legal limitations, on the UK mainland. Appointments are made on the IS exercise in exactly the same way, and for the same reasons, practice and assessment, as on other more traditional field exercises. A senior member of the staff told me:

'The general format of counter-terrorist operations has two great advantages for us, it produces a lot of potential for sending out small patrols which is good practice and with it many opportunities for making command appointments which are an aid to us in looking at individuals.'

The enemy for the IS exercise is made up of Regular soldiers dressed as civilians. It is a unique opportunity for them to throw bricks and bombs and generally abuse potential officers.[4] Tempers have been known to run quite high, and minor injuries (the inevitable result of realistic training) are not uncommon. For the Sandhurst students it is extremely valuable experience, as several in the past have found themselves on the streets of Belfast without further training (though normally those destined for Ulster must undertake a special preparatory course first).

A more traditional part of Sandhurst life is sport. The Academy either possesses or has access to facilities for almost every sport, including some of the finest playing-fields in Britain. Almost every team and individual sport is included. All students, when not otherwise engaged on exercise, must take part in a sport on Monday and Wednesday afternoons. The rationale behind this is that sport promotes fitness and confidence. These qualities are also promoted in PT. Army Physical Training Corps instructors encourage officer cadets and probationary officers to the required level of fitness. Training takes place in the gymnasium, on endurance runs and among the many vertigo-inducing delights of the Academy assault course. One should make the point that however daunting this may all sound, it is well within the capabilities of the average fit young adult. Those anticipating becoming students at Sandhurst are well advised to make sure they really are reasonably fit, as it will give them a distinct advantage. All Sandhurst students are taught to swim, and also have a free course of driving lessons if they do not have a licence. Those arriving at

[3] Counter Revolutionary Warfare.

[4] The WRAC have complained that they would like to take part in an IS exercise too.

Pull!

Sandhurst will find it useful — time being so short at the Academy — if they have these skills on arrival. During their vacations male students must undertake extra adventurous training, and many will qualify as UELs (Unit Expedition Leaders).

All students are taught how to handle the Army's principal small-arms systems, with the exception of the WRAC, who are only instructed on the pistol and submachine gun. After many years of deliberation the Army is introducing a new personal weapons system, the SA80 (Smallarms 80). This has necessitated the retraining of all Skill at Arms and Drill instructors. Male students will spend a great deal of time on the ranges improving their shooting skills. Both SMC and the graduates undertake a special 'live firing' exercise at Senny-bridge in Wales, on the edge of the Brecon Beacon training area. During this they practise basic platoon battle drills, firing with live ammunition. The training is of course extremely closely supervised.

Students attend a number of specialist presentations and lectures during their course. These are often given by outside experts. Subjects covered, usually in about an hour, include: alcohol and drug abuse, Army security, Army health and extremes of climate, the law of armed conflict (the Geneva Convention, etc.), assistance to the community, intelligence and the Soviet threat, public relations, the Territorial Army. A commander of a regular unit gives a talk on his experiences, and there is also another presentation given by a serving officer with combat experience, a recent one being given by Colonel Hugh Pike on his experiences with 3 Para in the Falklands. Once a year all students who happen to be in the Academy will attend the 'Kermit Roosevelt Lecture' given by a visiting three- or four-star

**Opposite:**

The assault course (*Central Office of Information*).

American general. Occasionally lectures will be given by members of British institutions such as the BBC. Recently a presentation was made by a senior policeman on terrorism and hostage-negotiation.

Students also have to prepare and deliver their own lectures, sometimes as individuals, sometimes as syndicates. Groups of students on all the long courses at the RMAS must present for study a talk about a famous leader who has been assigned to them. All students present, as individuals, at least one lecture on a hobby or topic of special personal interest. After giving their lectures they are debriefed on their performance by the instructing staff.

The Sandhurst Padre is responsible for organizing a short course, officially referred to as 'Christian leadership'. It considers the ethics of war from the Christian perspective, and all students of the SMC, SGC and the WRAC attend.

If what the reader has read thus far gives the impression that the Sandhurst curriculum is crowded, then that impression is not mistaken. As well as the subjects already mentioned, students are introduced to special language and methods of radio-communication at the Signals Wing. They are taught bare essentials of first aid, and the basics of administration, service writing and military law (the WRAC, as we have noted, do more of the office-related subjects than their male counterparts). As also noted in the previous chapter, students undertake some academic studies. These will no longer be significant in the case of the WRAC and the SGC, but the young men of SMC are to be introduced, for the first time, to Defence and International Affairs and War Studies.

Sandhurst courses are now so brief that they cannot hope to produce a young officer fully competent in the specific requirements of a corps or regiment. The course, rather, is designed to introduce students to many aspects of the Army, show them the Army way and how to fit in as an Army officer. One aspect of this is how to behave in the Officers Mess, and all students attend a representation of how not to behave. Although presented in a humorous manner, the point as far as the Army is concerned is meant in all seriousness. It might be summed up thus: don't be an oik, don't take tarts into the mess, show proper deference to senior officers and get a decent tailor. The Sandhurst staff I spoke to all felt slightly embarrassed by their role as social engineers, but defended what they believed was a necessity of maintaining traditional standards. The role model in all these endeavours might be described as 'upper middle class'.

A subject of great interest to those outside and inside Sandhurst alike is how students are assessed. The process begins, of course, before they ever arrive at the RMAS at Regular Commission Board, at a variety of interviews and at their medical examination. Most students will arrive at Sandhurst intending to go to a specific regiment or corps. For those who have not been 'badged' there will be more interviews by regimental representatives while at Sandhurst to see if the applicant is likely to fit in to their specific environment. Thus Sandhurst, in assessing its students, continues a process already begun, and one which is an ongoing fact in the lives of all Army officers. Each Sandhurst college has its own slightly different procedure, but the principles are common. As officer cadets and probationary officers are all too well aware, staff are watching them much of the time and exchanging notes on individuals. After major exercises, and at fixed intervals during the course, there are a number of college progress boards which consider every student. The college commander, the student's company commander and his platoon captain are present. The student's colour sergeant is not usually there, although he briefs the platoon commander. On SMC there are currently four progress boards with the option of a fifth to consider a very doubtful candidate at the end of the course. However, as well as the Progress Boards there are also 'Review Boards' which meet after the Progress Boards in the second half of the course to consider weak candidates, potentials for backterming, those with medical problems who through no fault may also be backtermed or 'Y listed';[5] and also the most successful students who may be promoted to the Cadet government and possibly even considered for the Sword of Honour.

No one is backtermed or asked to leave Sandhurst without the involvement of the Commandant himself. If someone is thought not to be pulling their weight they can be put on a warning. There is an escalating scale starting with a platoon commander's warning, going on to a company commander's and most seriously of all, to a College Commander's. What sort of thoughts go through the assessing officers' minds? One very experienced platoon commander told me 'Is the guy fit to be an officer? That's a very difficult question, because people change so much. We are talking about chaps of eighteen, nineteen, twenty, twenty-one — they're developing all the time. You have to project your reaction to them now to what they will be like in two years' time. Maybe he is missing a quality now, but one must ask oneself whether it will have developed sufficiently in two years' time for him to be okay.'

In New College, Officer Cadets are graded on a scale from A to E. It is not quite as straightforward as it sounds, for as well as the normal B plusses, C minuses etc, there are (but only for the letter C) 'C rising' and 'C lowering' on either side of C and in between C plus and C

---

[5] The Y list is a special category for students with significant medical problems. Once placed upon it students spend their time studying military history and international affairs and whatever else can be found to occupy them.

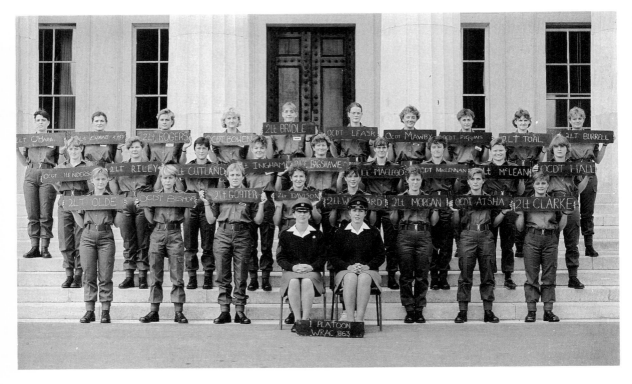

minus. They indicate an average candidate whose performance is going up or down. There is a D grade known as D(BT) which is an automatic backterming, and an E is an automatic ticket home. Most students pass out at grade C; anything above B is very rare. Sandhurst produces an aide-mémoire on leadership assessment for the use of staff. The basic qualities listed in this were first suggested by Field-Marshal Slim at an address at the Academy in 1952, they are: courage, willpower, initiative, knowledge and integrity. To these Sandhurst has added: self-confidence, enthusiasm, and the ability to communicate as "qualities of leadership" and as "additional important qualities": judgment and common sense, humanity, fitness, flexibility of mind, pride in command and faith. Students are also marked on the results of two professional knowledge exams, MK1 and MK2. They both contain questions on similar subjects — basic tactics, first aid, Army structures, map reading — but the second is slightly more advanced. Foreign students, although they receive as much attention, are not assessed as critically as potential British officers; indeed it is extremely rare for a foreign student to ever fail the Sandhurst course. The goodwill and in many cases financial contributions of their home states are extremely important to the Academy and to the Army.

A picture of this type is taken at the beginning of all male and female courses to assist staff in recognition. Second from right in the front row of this picture of One Platoon WRAC intake 863 is Princess Aisha, daughter of King Hussein (*Jim Farrar*).

# PHOTO-ESSAY

The photo-essay forming this section of the book took several months to complete and involved taking many thousands of pictures. The method is much the same as that used in some television documentaries, specific phases or events in the Sandhurst course becoming the themes for the various sections. No attempt has been made to follow a single company or platoon right through their training, although the eagle-eyed will note that some individuals appear more than once.

**Left:**
Already looking quite smart in track-suit order.

**Below and right:**
Physical fitness assessment in the gym.

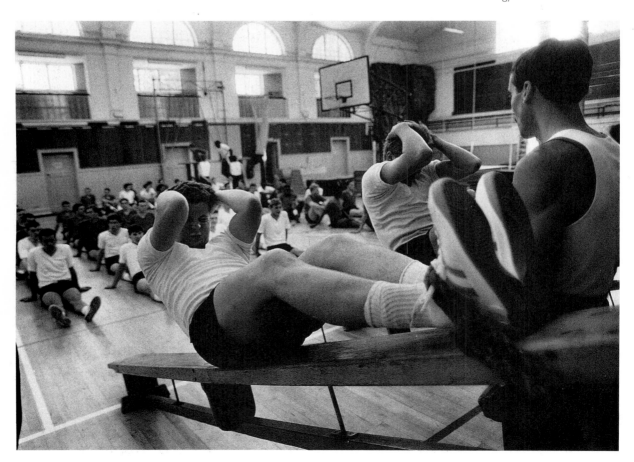

**Left:**
Colour Sergeant Harford's platoon.

**Right:**
Inspection.

**Below left:**
*! — *?!

**Below right:**
Fitness training!

'You weren't born, sir, someone . . . and the sun hatched you out.'

Even when cadets have completed the gruelling first five weeks of the course they have little time to relax, especially in their first term.

**Left:**
A helpful PTI offers some useful pointers.

**Opposite right:**
A graduate student officer in the classroom.

**Right:**
In the changing-rooms of the gymnasium.

**Below:**
A moment to relax.

**Right:**
'Bulling'.

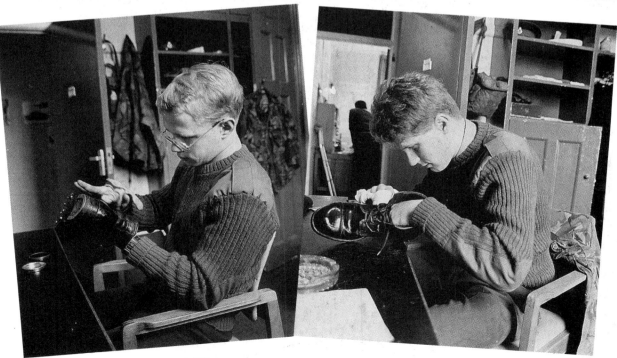

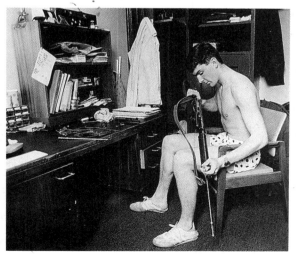

**Far left:**
Lunch.

**Above and left:**
Personal Admin.

133

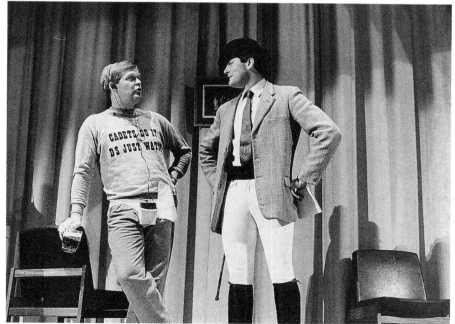

**Above left:**
A chat between periods in the corridor.

**Far left:**
Thinking ahead.

**Above:**
Putting weapons back into the Company Armoury.

**Left:**
A lecture on how not to behave in the Officers' Mess.

**Opposite and right:**
Getting acclimatized to an
APC (Armoured Personnel
Carrier).

**Below:**
Things could be worse.

**Left:**
Preparing orders.

**Right:**
'On Stag'.

**Left:**
'Digging in'.

**Above and left:**
'Personal admin in the field'.

**Left:**
Soft Option – Field HQ.

**Right:**
In command.

**Right:**
Preparing yet more orders.

**Below:**
Seeing if they work.

**Right:**
'When I get to London on Saturday . . .'

Helicopter drills.

**Above left:**
A member of the Directing Staff observes.

**Left:**
And more orders.

**Above:**

'When do I get my licence?'

**Above:**
Words of encouragement from the crew.

**Right:**
Gurkhas — Sandhurst's hard-working permanent 'enemy'.

**Opposite:**
The APC experience.

**Left and below left:**
Captain Lloyd tells it as it is.

**Below right:**
Testing.

Internal security training is now an important part of the Sandhurst syllabus, and one which most students said they found extremely interesting.

**Above:**
Learning to search a vehicle.

**Opposite and left:**
On patrol.

The WRAC learn to use the Browning pistol and the Sterling sub-machine gun during their training at Sandhurst.

**Above right:**
Princess Aisha 'squeezes one off'.

**Left:**
Fitness test.

**Above and right:**
In the classroom.

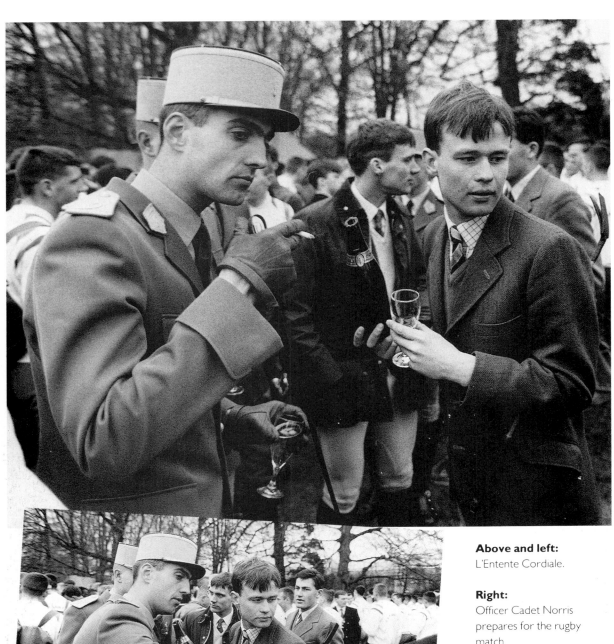

**Above and left:**
L'Entente Cordiale.

**Right:**
Officer Cadet Norris prepares for the rugby match.

**Above and left:**
'Vive le rugby!'

**Right:**
'Good Show'!

**Left and below:**
Tailors visit to measure for regimental uniform and civilian suits.

**Below:**
Checking No. 1 dress in good time for the Sovereign's Parade.

**Above:**
On the way.

**Right:**
A French veteran in Brittany takes the salute (the exercise was held in a part of France where the SAS and the French Resistance fought together.

**Left:**
Hearts and Minds.

**Below left:**
?????

**Right and below:**
In camp.

**Left:**
And yet more orders.

**Below left:**
Colour Sergeant Bedford compliments Officer Cadet and temporary Platoon Commander Henry Farr on the tea.

**Right:**
Officer Cadet Burgess in a thoughtful mood.

**Below right:**
Officer Cadet David Helm samples the local produce.

**Left and below:**
'Cammed-up.'

**Right:**
Washing it off.

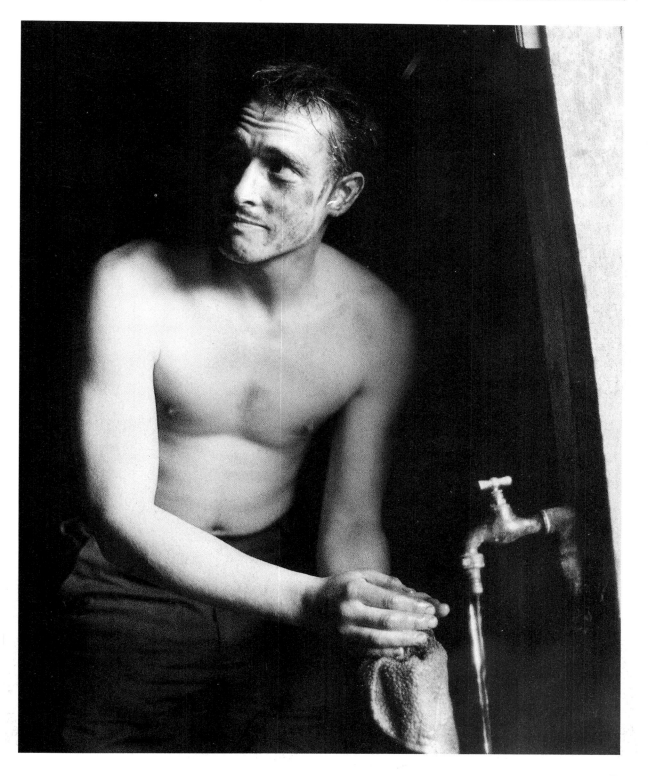

**Below:**
In the Chinook helicopter
going to the dropping-point.

The Battle of La Claie

**Right:**
Practising the 'de-bus'.

**Below right:**
Taking the bridge.

Fighting through the objective.

The enemy waits.

House-clearing.

**Above:**
The Adjutant prepares to mount ......

**Left:**
Directing guests.

**Right:** An Endangered Species – a member of the academic staff.

**Above:**
A record for posterity.

**Left:**
A well-known Princess, and
**right**, admirers.

The Student Officers and Officer Cadets
of
The Royal Military Academy Sandhurst
request the pleasure of your company
at
The Commissioning Ball
to be held at Sandhurst
on Friday 10th April 1987.

10.00 p.m.
Carriages 4.00 a.m.

Mess Dress, White or Black Tie.
Cash Bar                    (Please bring this invitation with you)

# POINTS OF VIEW

IN ORDER to give the reader a better impression of what is happening at today's Sandhurst, I include at this stage of the book a number of in-depth interviews with staff and students. They are presented in five parts. The first is devoted to interviews with male members of the Sandhurst military staff, the second to interviews with the young men on the Standard Military Course (starting with an interview with two recently joined students), and the third to interviews with members of the Standard Graduate Course. The fourth section consists of an interview with a female captain and a discussion with a group of female students, while finally there is an interview with a Territorial Army officer.

Where no full name appears at the beginning of an interview it indicates that an understanding to that effect was agreed before the interview started. Student interviewees were selected at random, except in the case of James and Andrew in section two and the young women in section four. In these cases the interviews were arranged for me by members of the staff on Sandhurst. I have used all the interviews made, and believe they represent a very fair sample, an opinion which is backed up by the common ground between them. The interviews have of necessity been abridged to remove excessive repetition and, at the request of interviewees, some grammatical errors have been corrected. Extreme care has been taken not to alter meaning in any way.

As far as the interviews with the male students are concerned, the opinions expressed were, frankly, rather more negative than I had expected. I suspect that this may be partly due to the extreme pressure those students find themselves under during their brief experience of Sandhurst. Being interviewed was a chance to articulate frustrations and irritations. However, that said, the criticisms made tend to be repeated by different individuals, and future planners may think this significant.

# THE STAFF

## THE COMMANDANT OF SANDHURST
*(Major-General Keightley, retired summer 1987)*

❝ The role of Sandhurst hasn't changed while I've been here: it is to develop leadership, and add a basic military knowledge as well. We don't attempt to give people a degree or a diploma like St Cyr, West Point or most of the military academies. They have the declared aim of training leaders for the nation, as well as for the Army. We concentrate on developing purely military skills. We get the intellectual requirements from our people in what they've learned as civilians. More than half the intake has already had three years at university. Certainly the Americans, when they visit, are most impressed by what we do. I would contend that our system is — dare I say it — better than theirs.

The Sandhurst academics were upset about ROTE because it removed the Regular Careers Course, which they really enjoyed, and the five weeks' worth of instruction they gave to the graduates. But the graduates said that the academic component was a waste of time; they hadn't enough time to absorb it and a lot of it was simplistic for them. This has changed to a two-week instruction given to graduates and non-graduates on very much the basics, "the Army and society". Instead of the RCC the academics — those remaining here — will run the Junior Command and Staff Course of four weeks, again the very basics of the subject.

The Military Technology Department has been closed because what it was teaching was pretty simplistic, covered a lot of ground that science graduates had already done, and was largely being duplicated by Shrivenham. Speaking personally, when I was here I did eighteen months, and apart from improving my maths and physics a bit it didn't stick. One wanted to get out and start doing things with soldiers, not wasting time. I can understand that academics not liking the correspondence course, but I did one for the Staff College and it got me through the exam very satisfactorily, thank you. The academic staff were often seen drifting about, under-employed, and nobody likes to be made to work harder. It was easier when Sandhurst was recreated after the war and the academics were almost to a man ex-soldiers. But once the three-year men arrived from Mons it was crazy to go on giving them two years' training with the atmosphere of a university campus.

Because the armed services have a rank structure, there has to be discipline between the ranks. There are enough officers in the officer class who want to live in the way people learn to live while they're at Sandhurst, so why should they all not live that way? In the senior NCOs mess, most of them have a way of living that they like, and they continue in that way. Why not? It compares quite well with what they would get at their level in civilian life. You've got to have a difference between the officers and the senior NCOs and that's where you get it. *If the soldiers begin to know their officers too well they also begin not to respect them.* We teach our cadets leadership, which is something the senior NCOs and

**'One wanted to get out and start doing things with soldiers, not wasting time.'**

**Opposite:**
*The Guardian,* 12 March 1984.

soldiers don't learn. They have to do things which the soldiers reckon are things their leaders are going to do: it's a question of perception. We're not trying to teach them to look down their noses at all communists and that sort of thing, but we teach them what would be expected of them in an officers' mess. In the show *South Pacific* there's a marvellous song called "You've Got To Be Carefully Taught"; it was applied to an American sailor not marrying a Filipino girl. You've got to get that right, and behave as the officers who you are with would expect.

The leadership aspect is latent in everybody, and in 95 per cent of cases it can be developed. The behavioural thing they can be taught, and those that need it love it. They feel that they have more polish, and in the eyes of a future employer they're more acceptable. Over the years the miners and the blue-collar workers have always aspired to doing better for their children, in order to move them up the social scale.

I don't want to see an Army officered completely by graduates. There are rather mundane, routine jobs which still have to be done by serving officers because they have to move round with the system, and an Army of nothing but graduates wouldn't give job-satisfaction to all its officers.

We're very sensitive to comments from the regiments here. The way we set up new courses was to send a questionnaire round to all the regiments and arms directors. We want to serve the customer, and just that. The Systems Approach to training — and I'm amazed it wasn't used years before — really means that you find out what the customer wants, work out how long it's going to take, and then plan your course; and there's a continuous checking system of feedback. It's very simple, really; it's what one should do all the time.

I never said we were benefiting society at Sandhurst: we're benefiting the Army. Sandhurst can't afford to be the philanthropic organization it once was. I would be delighted to do whatever the system wants of me. But my job is to teach people to be leaders and give them the basic training that they need to be officers in the Army. I'm not in the game now of developing leaders for the country. I still believe the things we teach them here about integrity, moral courage and leadership have great application outside. The country wants the Army to be straight down the line, dead honest, prepared to support whoever gives them their orders without any argument. I believe if one didn't get right at Sandhurst the standards for the officer class of the Army you wouldn't be able to maintain that. That's why it's so important that we make sure our officers have to be honest and upright, have moral courage and say what they really believe and not kowtow.

There are several aims in drill. It makes people react quickly, to jump to it. It builds up teamwork, and the one thing Sandhurst has always been good at is drill. One of the ways one builds up a Sandhurst spirit is in putting on a really good parade. It's also part of the build-up of self-confidence. People come here from many backgrounds, they need not necessarily have done anything particularly outstanding before, they may not be games' players. But they can be taught to do drill well, and they can be proud of themselves marching in front of their Queen

**'I don't want to see an Army officered completely by graduates.'**

or her representative. The cadets do enjoy the big parades, there's no doubt about it.

A lot of the problems for a Commandant are getting a feel for the place, public image and how you deal with certain small situations. We are an educational establishment. It's a very rewarding job, because in spite of the shortness of the course, and in spite of some of the rather scurrilous opinions the boys can produce after they have left, you do see the most enormous difference between the day they arrive and the day they go. Not just in the way they stand and the way they cut their hair but in many other ways. The things which one believes are important in the Army can be inculcated in these young men for continuation. **"**

## CAPTAIN DAVID FOXLEY, RE

**"** While I've been at Sandhurst I've been an instructor on Rowallan Company, on SMC, 2i/c on an SMC, and my final job has been running the RMAS spectacular [a military pageant].

There is a Sandhurst method. It's very difficult to define. It's throwing people into an environment in which they learn through their own mistakes. We let them make mistakes — at least most of us do! — we don't pounce on them. We do come down on them quite heavily if we consider it necessary for them as an individual, if otherwise they wouldn't learn. But we don't deliberately do so until the final parts of the course, because we consider that they should have learned the game by then. They should be able to provide the goods, or they go back or go out.

The method is to get them to learn something, put it into practice. If it's wrong we make them do it again in a different situation. All the time they're relating their experience to their contemporaries, watching them do the same thing. In a command situation one guy is nominated as a commander, that's his practice. If he does well he gets praised and all his mates know. If he does badly we explain to him, we always let them know what went wrong. He will get another go, and everyone else will store it in their memories and won't do that next time. Those are the two parts to it, that's the method. We teach everything through the vehicle of leadership. If the mistake is repeated over and over again they obviously haven't got the message. Usually a guy who keeps on repeating the same mistake isn't suitable. He'll be backtermed, and probably in the end will go off the course.

**'Usually a guy who keeps on repeating the same mistake isn't suitable.'**

The theories are important. It would be very difficult to teach leadership, a very intangible subject, without something to hang their hat on. I always try to refer it back to theory when I'm teaching. Whether the guys take them away with them I don't know. I know that as a cadet I learned the theories and forgot them all three minutes after I walked out of the gate, but probably it was at the back of my mind. I don't think they ever consciously relate to it again — unless they come back as instructors!

Leadership is a difficult subject to teach. It can be taught as long as the method is right, as long as you teach by example. You show somebody a situation and what would be a good method and a bad method of dealing with it. Then you put him into a situation where he has to effect a solution. Then show him what went wrong and what went right. That is the only method of teaching leadership. You can't teach it as theory, saying "he was a good leader, he was a bad leader". The theory seems now to be coming down from above to meet the Systems Approach idea. But that's a thing of the time. Any school of the sort that we have here [management/leadership?], including out in civilian life, is doing the same thing, trying to grasp what it is they are actually teaching. In the past there wasn't a lot of theory about it, they just "did it". We're probably justifying the means rather than anything else. There's value in it up to a point.

In the initial stages of training they only get the chance to command each other, and that's part of the method. They do something in an environment that is quite closely controlled. But on the final exercises we do let some of them command soldiers. The "enemy" is normally composed of a company of soldiers from outside, and some of the cadets will command them. But you can't afford to do that until the final stages of the course. Before that you'd be putting people into a position they weren't ready for: they'd have to exercise command and control over a bunch of people who look at them very critically but who are not really giving them any positive feedback, as other cadets do.

The course has been trimmed down to the absolute necessary foundation subjects in the last ten years. And in the last two years as we've done the rewriting for the new three-term ROTE course every single subject, every lesson, every five minutes that the cadets and the DS spend, has been critically looked at to ensure that it is totally relevant, something they have to know. Everything we teach now is very relevant to what they're going to do when they arrive in a unit. Take an exercise like a platoon attack. We've looked at it and said, if he's an Infantry officer he'll be taught that again when he leaves Sandhurst, and if he's a Sapper he might use it again, if he's in the RAOC, he won't. But still it is a very useful vehicle for teaching leadership. Obviously the cadets have to be seen to pass the course, but it isn't a rite of passage.

The course looks very much long-term. With any starter course like this you can't look too much into the future. But we're looking to the guy leaving here and becoming a senior captain. Once he does that he'll go on another course, the JCSC, and then on to Staff College. So we're providing a good foundation course for anything up to twelve years' service.

I think we *must* instruct people in how to behave as officers! The Army is an odd organization in civilian terms. We are very conscious of our behaviour, and that is accepted. We're very conscious of our traditions and the way we do things. I think it's important that we teach those things. In the past people were partially trained in those ways, brought up in a different environment; a lot were public schoolboys who were moulded in the same way that the Army likes to mould people. Now we're taking people from different levels of society. When they arrive at their units they'd be embarrassed because they don't conform,

'The course has been trimmed down to the absolute necessary foundation subjects in the last ten years.'

their behaviour might not be as required and they won't understand the traditions. It's more to save that than anything else, and to keep the traditions alive.

If the old system is shown not to work with new technology, then I think it will change. The Army has changed a lot in the last twenty or thirty years, and I don't see it stopping. It is a conservative organization and that's no bad thing, but it's not so conservative that it can't see the light. If changes happen that affect it badly it will change, I don't think there's any doubt about that.

The tradition of Sandhurst impressed me, and the fact that it's very much unchanging, despite all the changes we've had in the programme, the emphasis, the kind of person who is arriving here. Coming back to Sandhurst is very much like going back to the old school. Everything is very similar, very secure. As an instructor what is difficult is changing your job every couple of terms — quite unlike being in a unit. Other than that there aren't many things that I don't like. It's a very nice place to live and work, very beautiful with fantastic facilities, and that makes up for an awful lot.

It's difficult to cope with there being so many senior officers here. You learn to accept it. A captain — which is a fairly senior position in a unit — is given little responsibility here. But anyone who's been here a while just shrugs their shoulders and says "That's just the way it works." People are more career-conscious, across the Army, than they were a few years ago. I'm a Falklands veteran, and I notice that a lot of people who came back from there tend to shrug their shoulders about things like that. Life is very short, and you should make the best of it. There isn't a lot of time for messing about or being so serious about life that it becomes a bore. **"**

## COMPANY SERGEANT MAJOR ———

**"** I'm —— Guards, I've been at Sandhurst since the summer of 1986, and I'm thirty-seven years old. I like Sandhurst. We've got a programme that runs to the training programme, which is itself a good one. The personal administration is easy to do. We've got three extremely good colour sergeants, three extremely good captains, a good company commander. So anything you want to get done you can get done. I don't like the way it's over-administrated. There are lots of people in Academy HQ we never see who put a letter out and don't realize the problems they're producing. The hardest thing is the work — six days a week, with chapel on Sunday. You've never really finished a day's work, things still happen at six or seven o'clock in the evening. If there's a long period of time before a change I would probably receive six letters from everybody and his dog telling me about it. But I could be told on the telephone at twenty minutes' notice. If I was a cadet I'd think "What a stupid bloody system, why couldn't they have told us that before?" but I find out only ten minutes before they find out. That's the Sandhurst system. There are too many chiefs and not enough Indians.

I've very impressed with the vast majority of the cadets here. They're willing

'I don't like the way it's over-administrated.'

to have a go; unlike recruits, they're a breed unto themselves. The better ones bring on the weaker ones, so when they pass out they're all about the same standard. In recruit training and battalion life the strong rule and the weak are ruled, but not so here. If you're going to rise through the ranks to NCO it's very much survival of the fittest. But officers don't have that inbuilt burning ambition to take someone else's shoes. They are more friends together than we are. As NCOs and WOs you tend to be more aloof anyway. Here as a colour sergeant if you make one mistake you're out. Because of the high calibre of colour sergeant here, and because there are good people waiting in the wings to come here, and because the battalions and regiments treat this as a prestige posting, then if anyone does fall by the wayside it's time that battalion or regiment's representative is removed. They can't afford for people to be seen to be falling down. And that applies to private life as well; it's a large academy but it's a small place to live. **"**

## COLOUR-SERGEANT 'A'

**"** I came to RMAS a year ago, and this is my third term in New College. I'm thirty-three years old. A surprise was that the WO1 and WO2 ranks here were far more pleasant than others I've met. My own platoon commander is one of the better captains I've met. A couple of the company commanders are very good, a couple I wouldn't want to serve under, they're not the right types for this place. This is a thruster's job, and the old-established system can hold them in check.

I don't believe there's such a thing as a Sandhurst method. If you teach drill the way you learned it, by the book, nobody's understood what you've taught because it's just too "regimented" for them; so you relax and explain the same thing in a more natural way and the cadet picks it up a lot more easily. That's the Sandhurst way, the Guards depot way, and any good drill instructor's way.

Drill is relevant in any military set-up. Like it says in the good old book, drill is the basis of discipline, and provides teamwork. It's got a place in any army. The standard of drill that is taught here is very high, and this is reflected in the cadets' bearing. The drill syllabus here is about eighty periods in six months.

I was again pleasantly surprised by the attitude of the young cadets. There are some who are arrogant, ignorant and 'orrible, but the vast majority are very pleasant young men, very keen to learn, and thoroughly enjoyable to have dealings with. There is a proportion of State-educated cadets, from the same background as me, here. In my last platoon there was one kid whose father was loaded and so was the kid; he had pots of money to spend, he produced all the champagne and didn't mind what he paid. I discovered within a week of him passing out that he'd been taunting one of the State-educated kids whose parents had no money. You know, "You are a working class lad, what you doing here, how are you going to cope in the officers' mess?" It caused a lot of friction within the platoon, and the rich kid was very unpopular. Having said that, there was another kid who was probably equally as rich but didn't let it be known, who was one of the most popular people in the platoon.

'There are some who are arrogant, ignorant and 'orrible, but the vast majority are very pleasant young men.'

# No managing director makes tougher decisions.

Anyone who runs a business often has to make decisions that affect people's livelihoods.

But Army Officers make decisions that affect people's lives. This happens not just on the streets of Belfast.

As part of the U.N. Force in Cyprus, the role of the British Army is to keep the peace. Nevertheless, when Officers are giving orders to armed soldiers there is no room for errors of judgement.

Someone could end up dead.

Even on Salisbury Plain an anti-tank missile is still a lethal weapon.

This type of work can put quite a strain on a young man. His intellect, fitness, courage and sense of humour are continually under scrutiny.

We doubt whether business executives are allowed the same awesome responsibilities as an Army Officer.

And certainly not within twelve months of leaving school or university.

If you are aged between 17½ and 26 and you would like more information, write to Major John Floyd.

Tell him your date of birth and educational qualifications, and he will send you a booklet called 'Army Officer. What the job is like and how you can apply for it.'

Address your letter to Army Officer Entry (Dept. D58), Lansdowne House, Berkeley Square, London W1X 6AA.

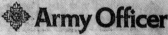

**Army Officer**

*Sunday Telegraph.*

We're brought up to be NCOs and we see our officers behaving like they do. And they are very good in the British Army, I think: for the most part the British officer acts like an officer, and well done him. So if we see a cadet behaving like he shouldn't, perhaps like an NCO (and some of them are ex-NCOs), it's easy for me to say "Hey, stop that, an officer wouldn't behave like that — think about it, and don't do it again." And the cadet will respond to this, because he knows that he's not behaving like what he wants to be. The difference is that we don't have to worry as much about integrity as officers. An officer can't be seen to be scruffily dressed, they've got to be well spoken, well mannered and well behaved. I don't think I know many NCOs who would prefer to have an officer who was the same background and spoke the same as them. In my own platoon was a kid who spoke the same Yorkshire as I do, and I went out of my way to get him to speak "posher". He was going to a Yorkshire regiment and it just didn't sound right. How could I let him loose on a platoon of Yorkshiremen speaking the same accent as them? They wouldn't respect him. If he behaves and acts and talks like you expect an officer to behave the respect's there straight away.

'The difference is that we don't have to worry as much about integrity as officers.'

There's a popular misconception among the whole NCO corps of the British Army that a guy who leaves here is a trained second lieutenant, a platoon commander. But they're not trying to teach them to be platoon commanders or anything about military tactics, they're just trying to teach them leadership. In six months the system teaches him to make decisions and be a leader, then away he goes to his Corps and they teach him the tactical or trade side of his career.

The platoon colour sergeant is the one seen by the cadets most. They look up to him, he is their mentor and everything he says is right. People need to be prodded in the right direction. That's one of the most fundamental parts of the job. If the cadets see him make a mistake the system has to remove him from their presence.

There are things going wrong at Sandhurst. It would take a long time to discuss it. It's obvious things are going wrong when the cadets who are being taught criticize the system. In a first-aid lesson I was given forty minutes to teach an introduction to fractures, and how to apply a bandage to any type of fractured limb. That tells me that the system considers first aid to be a low priority. But didn't the Falklands teach us that first aid is important? There were people who went to the Falklands straight from the Academy. There isn't enough time allocated to NBC warfare, either. I must say that, looking at the academic package, I'm not sure that it's what the cadet needs. This was an area where cadets were most vocal in their criticism. They'd say "What relevance is that to me as an officer?" and I couldn't help them. They were also critical about some of the tactics taught here. If you're teaching tactics obviously out of date you should say stop, and modify to the new tactics. You get fairly old officers here whose last minor tactics course might have been ten or fifteen years ago. I feel it's a young man's Army and the young men should be given a chance. A lot of back-stabbing goes on among the officers around here, and I don't think that's fair. Saying that, I am aware that officers listen to what I say, but they've got other things to consider. Colour sergeants do see life from their point of view and speak accordingly.

What I like most about Sandhurst — that's very difficult to answer. What I like most is the cadets, and not much else about Sandhurst is likeable. **”**

## COLOUR-SERGEANT 'B'

**“** I've been at Sandhurst now two years. To even do the cadre course[1] to get here you must have put in ten or fifteen years' service and have qualified as an instructor in first aid, at NBC, at section commander and platoon sergeant level at Breckon, at skill-at-arms, and they like you to have a certain amount of service in Northern Ireland or a similar field. You are then selected by your unit to do the Sandhurst cadre course, which lasts five or six weeks. The Sandhurst method exists, it changes with the times although it's slightly behind the latest infantry tactics. But the tactics are mainly a vehicle to look at the cadets' leadership.

The most important thing is the first few weeks. Bring them down to earth with a bang, let them know how little they know and how unimportant they are. But very soon after start giving them power, let them use their leadership abilities and their intelligence and see how it goes. The more rope you give them the better they become. I used to worry about them making mistakes because I thought it would reflect on me as platoon colour sergeant. For my first course I was very Guards-oriented — as I still am! — very conscious of discipline, and I kept them on a very tight rein. I slackened off a lot more on the second platoon and I found I enjoyed the course more. We do get some bad ones; however much you train them and bring them along they're never going to become leaders. Unfortunately, some of them pass out. To get someone to fail the course he's got to be particularly bad in discipline as well as in his leadership abilities.

'The most important thing is the first few weeks.'

When the course starts, for the first five weeks, you almost eat and sleep with the cadets. You come in at 0615 and stay with them right the way through until 2200 hours. But from when I was a lance-sergeant instructor at the Guards depot I've wanted to come here. Within the sergeants' mess at the Guards depot it's considered the next stepping-stone, if you come here as an instructor you're going to do well. But if you make a mistake you're on the "eleven o'clock train", returned to your unit. As colour ser'nts we are the lowest rank here, and the buck stops with us.

There are certain parts of the British Army that won't accept you unless you are from their social background because you have to fit in that regiment and officers' mess. The ones coming from the lesser backgrounds will only get into certain arms or corps. Coming from the Guards Division, where you need a certain amount of position and background to join, we do have a good inbuilt knowledge of it, and we do take some part in teaching the cadets to be officers. For example, I won't allow any swearing in the platoon lines by my cadets. The difference between an officer and a private soldier must be the way they conduct themselves, the way they dress, the way they handle themselves.

[1] The special course for would-be NCO instructors at the RMAS: see page 98.

# Find out if you're a leader before life forces you to become a follower.

How can you tell if you're a leader if no one's ever asked you to lead?

The answer, it seems, lies in the way you tackle little, everyday problems like the ones we pose below. Try them.

Are you honest? Do you show initiative? Good humour? Consideration for people in your power? If so you might make a good Army Officer.

Such qualities are far more important than the rather suspect desire to lead.

We're really looking for young men others want to follow.

**1. If your family is quarrelling about which TV channel to watch, you:** a. Go upstairs and read.
b. Argue vehemently for your choice.
c. Suggest everyone chips in 50p a week towards a video.

**2. On a walking holiday one of your friends dislocates an ankle, you:**
a. Try to reset it.
b. Carry him between you.
c. Make him comfortable while you ask the fastest runner to go for a doctor.

**3. You're dropped from the team in favour of an inferior player, you:**
a. Tell the coach to stuff it.
b. Try to convince other team members the coach is useless.
c. Impress him so much in training he has to pick you.

**4. One day you will:**
a. Buy up Richard Branson.
b. Have supper with Linda Lusardi.
c. Organise voluntary work in the Third World.
(Note: b and c are not mutually exclusive.)

**5. You run a small pop group but no one will give you a booking, you:**
a. Disband.
b. Try 6 more phone calls.
c. Find your own venue.

**6. As a prefect, you always make sure your boys:** a. Know who's boss.
b. Obey the school rules.
c. Are treated like responsible human-beings.

**PREFECT**

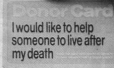

I would like to help someone to live after my death

**7. Realising that many people need organ transplants, you:**
a. Think the whole idea's macabre.
b. Have delayed a decision.
c. Become a donor and carry a card to prove it.

U S A

**8. An ideal holiday for you would be:** a. Dozing on the beach at Corfu.
b. Joining a package tour to Morocco.
c. Working your way across America.

**9. Which do you find most enviable:** a. The ability to predict currency exchange rates.
b. Chris Broad's batting.
c. The courage of Bob Champion.

**10. The threat of nuclear war prompts you:**

a. To join CND protests outside the American Embassy.

b. To write stiff letters to the Russians.

c. Spend part of your life in a peace-keeping force to prevent it ever happening.

**11. You would most hate to have the reputation of:**

'a. A fool. b. A shirker.
c. A bully.

**12. The prospect of commuting every day is:**

a. The price you pay for a settled life.

b. A chance to do a bit of reading.

c. Appalling.

**13. Your attitudes to computers can be summarized as:**

a. They'll never replace human intelligence.

b. Help!

c. It's a language you have to learn these days.

**14. You accidentally damage a parked car, you:**

a. Thank God no one saw you.

b. Clear off quickly.

c. Leave an apology and your name and address under his windscreen wiper.

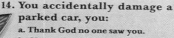

**15. Faced with the prospect of your daily run with friends the morning after a binge, would you:**

a. Forget it and lie in?

b. Lie in but pledge to run twice as long the next day?

c. Curse loudly but get up and run?

**16. At a party someone suggests charades which you hate, you:**

a. Say you'd prefer Trivial Pursuits.

b. Take part reluctantly.

c. Try to enthuse your team with original ideas.

**17. You realise that a natural leader would probably choose answer 'c' in most cases, you:**

a. Think 'what a wimp!'

b. Consider a safe job in insurance is more your line.

c. Think you may have leadership potential but realise it doesn't make you better, only different.

Don't criticize yourself if you're not perfect. We won't. In fact, we'd be rather suspicious if you were.

But if you feel you have a spark of leadership in you the Army will fan it into a flame.

One final question before we refer you to the coupon:

Soldiers have to know their leader would risk his life to save theirs.

Still interested?

We've a good relationship with the junior officers here. We treat each other with respect because they couldn't do our jobs, and we could possibly do theirs but not quite as well in certain fields. Job-satisfactionwise this post is first class, but statuswise we are doing a job beneath ourselves: in a normal unit we would be dealing with administration or training, while here we're doing a platoon sergeant's job. Sergeants are becoming more on an even keel with officers; an NCO now is far more intelligent and far more qualified than he ever was. The higher calibre of instructor must reflect in the end product.

I wouldn't be naive enough to believe that the chaps who come here don't know what they're letting themselves in for. They're given a dog's life at first, they are chased from breakfast to lights out. They have no privileges, they're not allowed electrical appliances, civilian clothes, to walk out of camp or drink alcohol. It builds up the team spirit very early on. Once you start releasing privileges back to them they appreciate them, and it produces a better man at the end of the day. The pressure increases but the discipline slackens off slightly after the first five weeks. I do consciously change my personality after that, but whenever they tend to get slack I'll beast them again.

What changes would I make in the course? I'd need to sit down and think about that. There are many minor programme changes I'd like to see done, but no major ones. The course, for what it is and the time it has, is very good. Nine times out of ten they produce a reasonable officer at the end of it. Particularly in the Guards Division, when you arrive as a young guardsman you are taught that the officer is one step down from God. When you come down here you realize that they're just recruits with a little more upstairs and a little more background.

'When you arrive as a young guardsman you are taught that the officer is one step down from God.'

One of the aims of drill is that it provides the basis of teamwork, and it makes them react under command. If you're in a trench, terrified, and somebody says to you sharply "Move!", that sharp command will be the thing that makes you move. I'd like to see a few more drill periods because they do rush what they have to learn. And the standards which Sandhurst expects can only be met if the platoon drill as often as they possibly can.

I went through a phase of thinking of becoming an officer, but definitely not now. Although the officer would get more pay, higher pension and more job benefits, there's no question in my mind that the NCO Corps of the British Army is now the highest calibre of any corps in the world. We are literally second to none. For my own personal pride I wouldn't change.

What do I like most about Sandhurst? The job satisfaction, the officer cadets. I don't like this establishment very much because it's definitely "Upstairs, Downstairs". If you can accept that, the job is great. But after you've been here a few months the class distinction which is here smacks you in the face. I suppose it always will be here because it's one of the things Sandhurst is geared on. It's acceptable because the way he handles himself is what makes the distinction between a young officer and a private soldier. I suppose I'm of an NCO class which is a breed all to itself. But no matter what we think Sandhurst will never change. Good men come and good men go, and no one is irreplaceable. **"**

# STANDARD MILITARY COURSE OFFICER CADETS

**Christopher.** I'm Christopher Roads. I'm twenty-three years old. I went to St Albans public school and the University of Bath. I graduated in July 1986 and came here in May to do SMC. My father is a director for the Woolworth holdings company.

**Richard.** I'm twenty-two years old. I went to grammar school in Cornwall, spent two years at Kingston Polytechnic doing an Earth Sciences degree, didn't finish the course. My father is a planning engineer.

**Christopher.** If you had to categorize, I suppose we're both middle class.

**Richard.** We've been at Sandhurst now for six weeks — it feels like six months. It's been really tough, to say the least. The first five weeks have been exceptionally tough. We both had a lot to learn, being civilians with no military background whatsoever coming into the Army.

**Christopher.** It was very hard work adjusting to Army life, getting up at half-past five in the morning, especially coming from college. The lack of sleep has made it very difficult to concentrate. If there's a lecture at half-past seven at night everyone falls asleep. It's mostly mental fatigue because so far the course hasn't been very physically demanding; it takes a long time to work up to the required standard of fitness. You wake up in the morning, first thing, and just think "Oh God, why did I come?" But as soon as you've had a couple of hours you get into the swing of it.

**Richard.** I came into the Army for job security — not many people get made redundant in the Army. I've fancied the Army since I was at school, particularly the Royal Engineers as I'm interested in the survey side. And I wanted to get out and about and see the world.

'I came into the Army for job security.'

**Christopher.** For me it was more that I'd done a desk job and just got bored to tears. I enjoy being outside and I enjoy the variety of Army life. You've got, say, live firing in the morning and cricket in the afternoon. I know it's a terrible cliché, but it is true.

**Richard.** We've got thoroughly hacked off while we've been here. In my third week I even went to see my colour sergeant because I was so depressed, tired and I'd had enough. I thought I'd better leave. He just looked at me, and, in his own words, said "Fuck off, come back another time". I wasn't going to argue. A couple of days later he asked if I was all right, and I felt a bit better, so he told me to just get on with it and it would get better. It hasn't!

**Christopher.** Three of us in our platoon had never stood to attention before in our lives, we didn't know what the hell was going on. You're expected to pick everything up the first time, if you don't get it right you're in trouble. It's very difficult to adjust to, but we're getting there. If anything it turns you the other way. You react against the military way and try to relax even more.

**Richard.** I don't think it's changed me at all, I still have the same outlooks on life. The only way it's likely to change us is physically. We're going to get fit one day.

**Christopher.** I selected my regiment after taking my degree. I was sponsored by the Royal Anglian Regiment.

**Richard.** Most people come here sponsored by a regiment but there's no pressure on you to stick with that regiment. You can change your mind if you want. We both did a pre-RCB which takes three days. I did mine with the Royal Engineers, and I did a familiarization visit at the same time, making it just less than a week.

**Christopher.** I'm not sure what Sandhurst is trying to do to us. Kill us? At the moment it's just trying to turn us into soldiers, changing us from a civilian to a military way of life, nothing more than that. Towards the end of the course it will try and develop our leadership as well. I'll never remember the 24-hour clock — what's 17.54? — and no one seems to speak English, everything's abbreviated. I

## NEW STANDARD MILITARY COURSE STRUCTURE

| TERM | STAGE | WEEK | CONTENT | SUBJECT COMMON TO ALL PHASES |
|---|---|---|---|---|
| **1** Basic Training and Leadership | **1** | 1 to 5 | Basic Recruit Training<br>Introduction to Organisation<br>Pass Off the Square | Leadership |
| | **2** | 6 to \|14 | Section and Platoon Battlecraft<br>Patrol Battlecraft<br>Oral Orders<br>War Studies<br>Comminication Skills<br>SELF RELIANCE Ex (Local Areas)<br>Ex LONG REACH (Sussex Downs)<br>Ex SARUM STEPPE (Salisbury Plain)<br>Ex HAT TRICK (Local Areas) | Skill at Arms |
| | | 15 | ADVENTUROUS TRAINING | |
| **2** Tactics and Assessment | **3** | 16 to \|21 | Advance, Attack, Defence, Withdrawal<br>Demolition Guards, FIBUA, NBC<br>Field Firing Battlecamp<br>Ex FIRST ENCOUNTER (Salisbury Plain)<br>Ex MARATHON CHASE (Stanford) | Signals |
| | **4** | 22 to \|29 | Counter Revolutionary Warfare<br>War Studies<br>Communication Skills<br>Ex DRAGONS TEETH (Sennybridge)<br>Ex BATON ROUGE (Longmoor) | Map Reading |
| | | 30 | ADVENTUROUS TRAINING | |
| **3** Officer Development | **5** | 31 to 44 | Training the Platoon<br>War Studies<br>Communication Skills<br>Contemporary Affairs<br>Military Technology<br>Platoon Administration<br>Range Management Course Stages 1–3<br>Military Law<br>Ex FAR FLUNG (Stanford)<br>Ex THRESHOLD (Overseas)<br>Ex HAT TRICK (Local Areas) | Drill<br><br>Physical Training |

find all the initials totally baffling. On the box — you had to laugh — it said "Pair of, one, George boots". They can't just say "one pair of boots".

**Richard.** It's not well organized here, far from it. There's so much pressure on you and so little time to do everything that you get problems with the timing. It *seems* very organized, but it's difficult to stick to the organization because of the pace life is led at here.

[Richard drops out at this point]

**Christopher.** Mixing with people from other school backgrounds works very well. Nobody's very different. Anyway, the school I went to only went public the year I went there; it was a normal State school before that. I don't have any problems that way, no one does.

The colour sergeant affects the whole mood of the platoon. One minute you can chat and laugh with him, the next he can be a complete sod. He really is the most important figure, more important than the platoon captain because we see more of him, he's with us twenty-four hours a day and he directs everything.

You need a distinction between officer and other ranks. You've always got to have a leading sect, and their training has to be different to that of the privates. If you try to break that down and everybody trains the same you're not going to have — it's an awful word, but an élite, leading the others. You've got to have that.

I feel very numb at the moment. You're so tired, you keep thinking this is a dream and you're going to wake up soon, but you never do. After the fifth week when we went home for the weekend I felt shattered. Even when I was awake I wasn't really awake. It was almost as if I was drunk or on drugs. Some nights you get three or four hours' sleep, and a 21-hour day. That's really hard going. It's hard work, yeah.

**PAUL** ——— *19 yrs old, completed SMC Course 1987 going to Royal Corps of Transport*

❝ I'm middle class, I suppose. My father was a staff sergeant, then a sergeant major in the Army. I went to the Gordon Boys School, not far from Sandhurst itself, and eighty to ninety per cent of the fathers of students there are in the Forces. More than anything I'd say family background made me decide to become an officer. My whole family since my great-grandfather have been military in some way or another. Looking at employment and how difficult it is to get a job nowadays, I thought — well, there's more security, more variety, more adventure than any other job I could think of at the time. And through my father I had first-hand experience of what the Army is all about. I decided to join when I was a young teenager. From the Gordon Boys School I did a Welbeck assessment board — very similar to the Regular Commissions Board, but all we do is academics. I'm going into the Royal Corps of Transport, it's my father's and grandfather's Corps.

Sandhurst was very varied, enjoyable, sometimes a right pain, especially in the first few weeks — they put you right off being in the Army. But once you're over

**'More than anything I'd say family background made me decide to become an officer.'**

209

that the pace settles down and it's like starting a new course. Once you get over the pressure — well, looking back at it it's excellent, it's really done something to me, I've learned something more about myself, how much more I can cope with. Each platoon is a very big team, everyone wants everyone to get through — without the help of some of them I would never have got through, and others will say the same.

I wasn't a "blade runner" — that's someone who tries for the Sword of Honour. That's what you're told to strive for, everyone has a vision "God, I'd love to be up there carrying that sword when the day comes round". But to actually achieve it you've got to be something special, I feel. You've got to shine above everyone else. You'd expect the Regulars, who've been in the Army before, to do that. But, quite surprisingly, I'd say there's always someone there, managing to pull you through. He's the bloke you go to for help. I wouldn't say he's any more intelligent, he's just more switched-on. My career in Sandhurst was average. Your ultimate goal at Sandhurst is to pass out. The Sword of Honour is a bonus if you get it.

We're told when we go there, "You're going to make mistakes, make no bones about it; you'll be punished for them but next time you'll know not to make that mistake." I think it's very fair in that way.

There was one person who was backtermed because his platoon commander — although perhaps it's not right to say it — had a very great dislike for him. Otherwise, those who were backtermed maybe needed an extra term. There was actually one person in our platoon who volunteered to go back in the last week of the course; he felt he needed extra time there. They are possibly better officers for having learned about it all over again, more knowledgeable. They crammed too much into seven months, and I think it's a good thing moving on to the year course. But looking back I wouldn't have liked to do any more. I feel competent that I know the rudiments of leading men. But we've heard from the Regulars who say how much different Sandhurst is — everything's there when you want it, but in a unit it's very difficult to come by certain things.

You are pushed to your limits so you learn just where they are, and you get to extend them, in fitness, courage, morale, confidence — you go up and up and up at Sandhurst. Confidence is one thing it really builds up, and it helps you when you're out in civvy street. Sandhurst has developed me in both character and maturity. There's no room for immaturity at Sandhurst.

You did have the odd few who tried to buck the system because they didn't agree with certain ways of doing things. But if you look at it closely there is a reason for the way they do it. Although you're told to go your own way and lead your own life there, they try to mould you into that sort of character, a Sandhurst character. They can stop you from doing something your own way and say, "No, you'll do it this way." When we went battle shooting, you decided on what you were going to do, and you said, "Right, I'm going to go left flanking on this attack." They said, "No, you're not, you're going right flanking." The ground on the left is a hell of a lot better to go by — more concealment, easier to move

'I wasn't a "blade runner" – that's someone who tries for the Sword of Honour.'

round on, you don't have to go through that silly river. But, "No, you'll go right flanking." You're restricted to the ways they want to do things. Within their bounds, you're okay. If you strive outside those bounds, they'll get a grip on you and tell you to do it their way, which sometimes I disagree with. I feel they should let people do it their own way. If they do it well, all well and good. If they do it badly then tell them not to do it that way again. The system is a bit inflexible.

I think the system is trying to mould leaders, giving you the basics on how to lead men. It can't go any further than that really. But you're commanding other leaders, so it's a bit of a farce in a way, but you'll find that at Sandhurst the students are very mature about it, they help those in command to do well, they advise each other. When you're leading a platoon at Sandhurst they know what you're doing and they can advise you not to do it wrong. When you go to your unit all your men will just sit back and let you do it, because they won't know any different. I think it all boils down to leadership, that's all the men below you are looking for. Leadership is — well, you've stumped me on that one! Leadership is the ability to get your men to do the thing you believe is right in the way you want it done. It's a matter of integrity, flexibility; they impressed upon us that moral and physical courage are two different things.

What was it like looking at myself on TV? Looking back on it, it all helps to build up confidence. Communications Studies was a valuable aid for me.

Sandhurst is just another factory. Someone goes in one end and out comes another stereotype. But there's more freedom at Sandhurst, they mould you in such a quick time that you attain a certain level and they can push you no further. Whereas at West Point or Saint-Cyr you're there for three or four years and they can mould you exactly the way they want you to be, so everyone leads in the same way. But when the American cadets came over you'd think they'd all be the same as each other but they all seemed to have their point of view still; so did the cadets at Saint-Cyr when we went over there. It's amazing the variation in character you still see. But their way of leadership is all geared into one mould.

What we look at is who's going to benefit us in the long run, the left or the right? My political views are just slightly right of the centre, because they benefit us most. Cash is important to me, it was one of the reasons for joining, but mainly I don't want a nine-to-five job where I get no variety. This way I get financial security and a bit of adventure. Who would turn it down? There's so much you can do in the Army, and you're totally secure financially as well. What would I be if I was in civvy street?

**'My political views are just slightly right of the centre.'**

There's usually some underlying factor behind it, but the majority of cases of hardship, it comes down to the people themselves. It's a very biased viewpoint, but that's the way I've been brought up. I've been given the opportunity to build on a good education — it's almost snobbish, really, the way I'm saying it.

Nuclear war? It worries me to death. I just hope I'm under it when it goes off. But more than anything it's a deterrent. The approach of the Peace Movement just isn't realistic. They may know the consequences, but if they knew the reality, and just how good a deterrent nuclear weapons are — but they're not prepared to listen to that. Should there be an all-out nuclear war there won't be much left.

The idea of killing doesn't bother me if it's to maintain peace. Those who are killing would inflict a hell of a lot more damage than I would on that one man. There are no rules to war. So long as you can maintain peace as quickly as possible whichever way you do it, I feel, is the best way. The end justifies the means. The warfare we have to deal with now is all to do with terrorism, and I feel the Sandhurst Internal Security training is a valuable aid. I don't see the point in terrorism. Take Northern Ireland, for instance. Just so they can have their own government they'll go around killing all the British who are trying to keep peace there. I think it's totally pathetic. I see no point to terrorism whatsoever — there has got to be a better way. The sooner we can stamp out terrorism the better. It never will be completely eradicated, but the more we hinder them, then hopefully the less and less it will get.

We knew all about Sandhurst's prestige. I was looking forward to going there, and from day one looking forward to completing the course, to be able to say "I'm now Sandhurst-trained, I've passed out of Sandhurst, can you match that?" It's not just a boast — the rewards at the end of it are absolutely superb. Everyone just couldn't wait to get out of Welbeck and go off to Sandhurst. But Sandhurst is — different. I'll put my foot right in it, I'm sure, but . . . it's not as well organized as I thought it would be, put it that way. You expect everything to go as planned, but in my first two weeks there we had about three or four programme changes, and that went on and on all the way through Sandhurst. They can never seem to get it right. So, I feel organization at Sandhurst leaves a lot to be desired — but I'm sure it does in any unit.

I'd seen the glossy advertisements to be an Army officer, but it wasn't those that made up my mind, it was my careers officer at the Gordon Boys School, and my father as well. I just had to look at those people in his unit, which I had the first-hand opportunity to do when he was a sergeant major. Do I think of myself, now I'm an Army officer, as a special person? Yes, I do. I don't think there are many people nowadays who can brag that they'll have over thirty men and millions of pounds worth of equipment to look after, especially at the young age of late teens to early twenties. But I don't see why I should change my class just because my status has increased. I'll always be middle class. I don't think I could cope with being upper class, financially and in such ways as that. Although I'll have to live a life like that, I know I'll always be middle class. There were upper-class people on the course, I got on well with them. Despite the fact that they're the same ones with thousands of pounds and a massive bank balance, I think you ignore that fact. You're all there with one aim, to pass the course. There were people on the course who were even, well, lower-class than me, and I don't worry about that.

The officer makes the ultimate decision, although he'll have many ideas on how to do it from the senior NCOs. I'm sure a senior NCO could do it just as competently as an officer. But you'll never see a smooth continuum from private

**'We knew all about Sandhurst's prestige.'**

**Opposite:**
*The Observer*, 10 October 1982.

# Mission impossible?

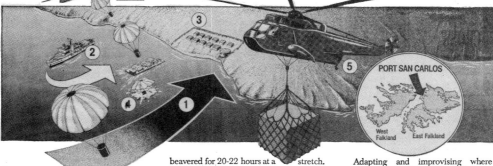

We'd never faced a challenge quite like the Falklands before.

Not so much the fighting. (We've seen our share of that in the past.) But the sheer logistical effort of going to war in one of the most inaccessible spots on earth.

Simply shipping out troops was a daunting enough prospect.

Combining with the Royal Navy and Royal Air Force, sending out combat supplies, setting up stores and opening supply lines was a task of unprecedented proportions.

In the event, it was a clear illustration (if ever one was needed) that wars aren't won by front line troops alone.

But equally by the men behind them.

Primarily in this case, the officers and men of the Royal Army Ordnance Corps (RAOC) and the Royal Corps of Transport (RCT) and the Corps of the Royal Electrical and Mechanical Engineers (REME).

**The unsung heroes.**

As in any conflict, these logistic troops were among the first into action.

Within 72 hours, the RCT had loaded over 15,000 tons of combat supplies on to ships of the task force ready for sailing.

It was just the start ① of 8,000 miles hard slog. Because as battle plans developed en route, most of these supplies had to be manhandled and restowed.

Not once, but twice. To ensure that each item was in the right place, on the right ship for the right unloading sequence.

When the ferrying ashore ② finally got under way, it became virtually a non-stop operation.

In San Carlos Water, all three Corps

beavered for 20-22 hours at a stretch.

Up to their knees in freezing water and under repeated attack from enemy aircraft, the men snatched what sleep they could on their Mexeflote rafts.

To say they carried us to victory, would be no exaggeration.

**Securing the beach-head.**

Within hours of the first assault, the commando logistic regiment (with men from these three main Corps) was ashore, paving the way for a supply base. ③

The RAOC then had the mammoth task of running it.

Covering an area of six acres, it had everything carefully located and logged – from ammunition (in half-a-dozen separate areas) to compo rations to lavatory paper.

Roads were built in and out of the base. And a traffic system devised to speed the flow.

At the same time, ④ men of the Air Despatch Squadron RCT were flying in high priority supplies. And organising mail drops on a daily basis. (Nothing keeps up morale more than a letter from home.)

On the ground, the issue and loading of supplies never faltered. By day, helicopters (the main form of transport) were crammed with food and ammunition for the front. ⑤

By night, Mexeflotes were piled high for the 'milk run' supplying troops based around San Carlos Water.

**Pushing on to Port Stanley.**

Without the skills of the REME too, even more stores and equipment would have been called for.

Demands that would inevitably have slowed down the advance on Port Stanley.

In appalling conditions and often under enemy fire, the REME carried out running repairs to front line equipment.

Adapting and improvising where necessary to maintain vehicles, helicopters, weapon systems and radios.

Their heroics, along with the rest of our troops', brought this tribute from the Minister of State for the Armed Forces:

"The British Army is manned by the finest professional soldiers in the world… people who will endure any hardships and overcome any discomfort to perform their duties regardless of the odds against them."

**Inspiring or frightening?**

If you've been considering a career as an Army Officer, all this may well have opened your eyes.

Perhaps you'd never realised the vital role of these three Corps before.

Their exploits rarely make the headlines. (Unlike those of our front line troops.)

But for all that, their tasks are none the less challenging or involving. And are just as important in peacetime as they are in war.

Perhaps you'd never realised either, what might be expected of you under pressure.

Could you have responded as positively as our young officers (many in their early twenties) in the Falklands?

You'll never know until you're tested. But if you feel you may have the mettle, we'd be delighted to hear from you.

Write to Major John Floyd, Army Officer Entry, Dept. A82, Lansdowne House, Berkeley Square, London W1X 6AA.

At this stage, all we ask is your date of birth, your educational qualifications and a few details about yourself.

Asking the impossible comes later.

to general. An officer has to have certain qualifications, he needs more intelligence, more initiative, he's more knowledgeable about certain things than a private. There'll always be that distinction between an officer and the junior ranks. The officers have the responsibility, and the senior NCOs are the technical experts. They know how to run something, but you're the one that tells them what's to be done with it.

Although he didn't say it to me, my father was very proud that I managed to get through the course. Sandhurst is a lot different from a unit, so all he could tell me was how his unit worked, and I had to gear my principles around what I'd been told by him. Otherwise, we were told by the Directing Staff what was expected of us, what we had to do and how we had to do it. The Directing Staff were almost gods to us.

The girls were a respite. Some of them are very interesting to talk to, but how people make relationships at Sandhurst I don't know. More girls are straying from mainstream WRAC to join the various Corps. But basically we're infantry soldiers at Sandhurst and you don't get the women for the infantry work. But if they divide Sandhurst into Corps so they can teach them a specific trade while they're there, we may see complete integration.

I've got A Levels in Maths, English, Physics and General Studies, all Grade E. I suppose I could have gone to a university or polytechnic, if they were desperate for someone. But I don't regret not going there. I wanted to get all my learning out of the way. I wanted to get out into the big wide world of the Army and actually do something that was worthwhile. Although doing my studies I was getting towards my goal I wanted to reach it as soon as possible, and going to university wouldn't have helped. Maybe one day I might go there, when I've settled down a bit. **"**

**'My father was very proud that I managed to get through the course.'**

### OFFICER CADET JAMES ——— *SMC Course*

**"** I'm nineteen, hoping to go into the RAOC. I'm working class, grammar school and Kingston College of Further Education. I went straight from that into a Potential Officer Course, and into Sandhurst.

I was as pleased as punch to finally get to Sandhurst. I was in awe of it, you hear so much about it. But as time wore on I realized there was nothing special about it. For me, it's just a place to learn a trade and get away from as soon as possible. There's a myth of Sandhurst that built up in my mind, and I'm sure when I leave I'll help continue it, but not now while I'm here.

The course is what you make of it. It can be tough if you want to work hard at it, or it can be quite easy if you have the ability and want to get through in the "grey area", unnoticed. I made it hard because I was conscious of my social background. I felt I had more to prove than the rest of them. The Cavalry and Infantry are mainly public schoolboys, and the Corps guys are mainly middle class, or those like me with high aspirations. Sandhurst is definitely middle class, there's very few guys like myself, with a South London accent, and not many upper class. The class thing shows in the way that the Cavalry and Infantry tend to stick together, and so do the

Corps guys. I've found it frustrating, I'm always conscious that I have to prove myself when guys can sail through the course with apparent ease based on background and attitude. They're very brash people; you tend to feel put down.

The first five weeks were very rushed. After that it settled down, but there was still a lot of pressure. I'm treated just the same as anyone else, maybe just a bit special because of my background. I'm representing the Academy at West Point next week. At the start I took foreign students under my wing, I supposed they rewarded me for putting effort into the place.

I'd never really had the opportunity for things like the mess presentation. It's still strange, but I'm picking up the trade: when to stand up, sit down, how to hold my glass, all etiquette. It's a learning process for me as it's all new.

My parents are as proud as punch, my mom can't stop talking about me. Where I come from no one else is an Army officer. Everyone wants a photograph of me in uniform. I was the first guy from my school in twenty-six years to go in as an Army officer. I was in the CCF [Cadet Corps Force] there, I worked up to acting CSM, which is the highest cadet rank. I quite enjoyed it. There's a definite change coming over my attitudes. My voice is changing; before I had a really broad cockney accent. I suppose I'm developing middle-class values really. I'll always be conscious of where I come from, but like anyone if you want to get on and do well in life you've got to make the changes. I've come into contact with a new peer group, I've got new responsibility, Sandhurst does actually set you in the right way. The Army doesn't demand that you change, but it is class-orientated and to do well in it you have to be part of the system. There's no point in rebellion. The reason why you joined was discipline, anyway.

The old distinction between officers and men is changing. Some of the men are more intelligent than the officers now. My idea of an officer is to lead from the front, to do a good job, to show the men you're doing a good job, and to include them. To do that you have to get to know them better. The image of Army officers in cartoons and on TV — that just doesn't happen any more. Because of technical changes you're working closer with the men, and it's no longer a case of "He's in charge, follow him!" You have to earn their respect. It's still "Sir", you are in charge, but officers and men can do a job together competently. Nowadays the men can become officers as well if they want to work at it, and most of them — especially in the technological side — will have the intelligence to do so.

Certainly I am frightened of having to deal with a platoon in the outside world. I know my peer group here, and they make allowances. Out there will be thirty guys who've been in the Army for five or more years, and I think they'll resent an officer fresh from Sandhurst telling them what to do. You don't learn the relevant skills here. For the next two years I'll still be learning, I won't have any command.

I normally vote Conservative. My dad has changed for this election [1987] from thirty-odd years of voting Labour to Conservative because he thinks Mrs Thatcher's done the country a world of good — and I've worked on him for the past ten years! I'm a career-minded person and I want to do well for myself, and I feel Conservative is best for that. If a Socialist government said they were going to

**'The old distinction between officers and men is changing.'**

disband the Army I'd be pretty upset. But I don't think the country would allow that, and if I got kicked out of the Army the fact that I've been to Sandhurst would stand me in good stead for a career. There's been a change in the country's attitudes over the last seven or eight years. We're more proud as a people than we were, we want to do better, the country has gone more right wing. From the age of ten I remember the Winter of Discontent and strikes everywhere. Now it just doesn't happen. Now the country wants to do well for itself, and that's what I'm a soldier to protect. I protect their freedom of choice.

What I've enjoyed most about Sandhurst is the social experience away from it. My peer group is builders, plumbers, labourers, brickies, and I'm in a sense one up from them, but I don't treat them as such. They're still my friends. I went to a friend's wedding a few weeks back and the DJ mentioned that I was an Officer Cadet. There were gasps and sighs and everyone turned round to look, I felt immensely proud, the effort I'd put in to get here was paying off.

I used to see a girl a couple of years ago and we're still friends. She'll be coming to the ball. I've started seeing a WRAC lady here as well. I like to keep my options open.

I'll miss Internal Security, which is a pity because it's the best exercise here. The way we're taught is good. We have the information. I remember more from the field than from theory taught in the classroom. Most of the stuff was taught in the first five weeks, and guys were falling asleep in their chairs. You can relate to theoretical models of leadership, it gets you thinking, and I like that sort of stuff having done Sociology A-Level. That's where I got "peer group" from.

I'm not concerned about the possibility of war. The first reason I joined the Army was to pick up a career, the second was to defend the country, because I'm quite patriotic, whereas some people here think of it just as a career. I'd be proud to fight. I'd like to go to Northern Ireland, get a red beret or serve in the SAS. And later on I can make use of the Ordnance by a career like bomb disposal. Everyone in the Corps is very career-minded, if you just want to join the Army you join the Infantry and learn nothing.

**'I'm not concerned about the possibility of war.'**

Extending the course is a very good idea. But they'll probably pack out the extra term with more stuff so you're still cramming it all. You learn enough here for the aim of the course. The extra time should be used to ingest it. I wanted to learn how to horse ride and clay-pigeon shoot but I never had the time, I was always on the go. I'm a "blade runner", I want to do well and to be seen to do well. If I feel I'm not noticed I'm quite downhearted, but I keep going. To anyone else I'd say, stay in the grey. If you're too good they'll want more, and if you're too bad they'll keep pressuring you. Sandhurst is your last stumbling block, once you're through it and in the Army you'll be looked after. Sandhurst is a minor public school where the cadet force has gone mad. ”

## OFFICER CADET ANDREW ——— *SMC Course*

“ I'm twenty-one years old. I came to Sandhurst in January and now have eight weeks to go before I'm commissioned. I went to Marlborough public school. I've no military background, my father's a seed merchant in Chester. I'm going into 5th Royal Inniskilling Dragoon Guards.

Obviously you only remember the good times, but it has been enjoyable and it has come up to my expectations. From watching documentaries like "The Paras" I expected it to be a lot harder than it is. There's so much classwork to fit in that they can't tire you out too much or they'd get a negative response. I wouldn't have liked it any physically harder. I find a greater sense of achievement doing much more practical things with an aim at the end. After a six-mile run you've just got hot and sweaty, you haven't achieved anything. The academic side is a lot easier than work I've done. We do have contact with the lecturers in Communications. I believe there's a hell of a back-up in the War Studies department here but we come across them only very briefly. We were given a couple of lectures on the Zulu War and Waterloo, but purely from a leadership point of view.

I know quite a few members of the WRAC but they prefer SGC because they went to university, SMC give them the impression of being little boys, they've just come out of school. SGC are twenty-one or twenty-two, with experience of life and a pip on the shoulder. I don't resent SGC, but I'd like to know what they're doing over there; they're kept so much away from us. It's chucked at us on arrival that SMC is the proper military course and they're covering something to train them for higher ranks, above major, so the aims of the courses are different. We're being taught to be soldiers and they're being taught to be desk officers.

I can't say whether I've changed at Sandhurst. My father, and my sister who's at university, reckon I've become far more pleasant and easy to talk to, and I stand up straighter. The training here, in the massive Army system, is orientated towards raw recruits. We're taught lessons that are recommended to take 45 minutes, and because we're slightly brighter it takes us about 15 minutes, so you get half an hour in which not much is taught and a lot of questions asked. More of the work should be orientated towards our level. It doesn't take forty-five minutes to show you what a rifle is.

The "gentleman syndrome", the officers' mess presentation, I find perfectly acceptable. There are social rules that one must abide by, and that's the way I've been brought up. Those who haven't do find it amusing, but because they're here they accept it very quickly. It's easy to walk out of here with your nose in the air, but you do feel much more proud of yourself. Your status doesn't increase as an officer, but you are a different person from your friends, and that's nice to feel.

'There are social rules that one must abide by, and that's the way I've been brought up.'

In my experience DS, the platoon sergeant and captain, are rather distant. They aren't really allowed to get amongst us and make friends, although there are one or two favourites. The platoon sergeant I didn't find at all daunting. On first meeting you work out what sort of person he is and how far you can go — is it just one big show? Invariably it is. No person can act like that the whole time, there is a normal self. He did frighten me in the first weeks because I'd never come across anyone like that before. He was shorter than me but sounded a hell of a lot louder.

The thing I've enjoyed most here is meeting people of a similar social background. Not that there's many of them any more. People in the platoons from public schools will congregate together, not during work, but in the evening they'll go to the same pubs, and they all know the same people. It wasn't a shock to meet people from different backgrounds, but it was a surprise how many backgrounds there were. I expected a lot more people who wanted to be an officer to come from a public school. Obviously, coming from a public school is an advantage in wanting to be an officer. You have a certain basis of discipline in a boarding school, you've had to motivate yourself for five years, and there are certain customs a school has which you have to follow. There are a lot of similarities between a public school and Sandhurst.

> '**I expected a lot more people who wanted to be an officer to come from a public school.**'

The thing which irritates me here is being treated like a child. In the first term they've got to mould you, and you haven't got a lot of freedom, so they've got to treat you that way just to get you into the routine. If they didn't you'd start thinking about what you're doing here. If everything is done for you then you follow very easily. It's rather degrading. It does give you a communal spirit in that everyone automatically hates it and starts pushing against the DS, which is probably the plan.

Mine is a short-service commission. I haven't really thought about my chances of seeing a war. Luckily it will be nuclear war, as I'm in the tanks. I won't be sent to Northern Ireland. In nuclear war you do your job — it sounds a bit corny — but the average time we'll last is seven days. You face facts that you're going to die. But it's comforting to know that everybody else is too, that's what motivates you most.

The morality of soldiering today is based on history. Men are always going to be jealous of each other, everybody fights for themselves, and you've got to follow that tradition, to protect yourself. The Army is just a centralized extension of this, you're protecting the common interest. My friends and I are aware of the threat of civil order breaking down in this country, maybe tomorrow. My TA role was in home defence and we were trained in anti-riot. I think it's likely that we'll get a replica of Northern Ireland here, in the lead-up to a war when outsiders come in and try to stir up riot, and it's the duty of the Army to help the police. We're starting on that kind of counter-revolutionary training now. I find it a lot more interesting than the basic stuff, because you've got to think of so many aspects: the law side, working with civilians. It's different from "bang, you're dead".

On politics, as a junior subaltern you're under the control of the powers that be. Just as a hypothesis, if a very anti-military Labour government doesn't want an Army it doesn't want an Army, and you're out of a job. If we were to leave NATO I'd think it was a bloody stupid thing to do. I don't think the peace movement, CND, is a realistic proposition. It's a minority which has encompassed the more narrow-minded members of the population, who haven't stood back and looked at the situation from a positive point of view. They're really completely loopy. They feel they have to fight for something, but what they're doing is a little out of their depth. Sitting outside Greenham Common is going to achieve bugger all. I'm pretty sure they're manipulated, told by informers what's going on — how else do they know where a nuclear convoy's going to be?

I've never had to defend my views as an officer; the people I do meet are not the sort to follow CND. If it came to it I would stick to my guns, but in this place they do change your views so much towards the pro-military point of view, and one does sometimes have to fight a bit. The split in politics today is bad because it works against everyone. As soon as you have a disagreement you automatically follow the side which supports the Army view. The trouble is you have to take with that all of that side's other ideas as well. I don't think you can be a Socialist and an Army officer. Your ideas wouldn't fit into the way the Army goes about things. We don't think about politics much, we follow in the footsteps of our parent. People want things to stay as they are now, all my friends are perfectly satisfied with the way it's going socially. Everyone likes to jump a social scale and no one likes to drop one, so you've got to keep it even. If you've lived in the middle of Birmingham all your life and your job is to sell papers then you're happy, that's your world. But I don't want to sound snobbish, I've really a very open mind. When you get down to friendship there's basically no difference. Sandhurst doesn't make you snobbish because you come down to the average here, and the average is much more middle class than I thought it'd be. **"**

Prince Charles presents the Sword of Honour to Officer Cadet Nick Oliver, December 1978, (*Keystone*).

# MALE GRADUATES

### SECOND LIEUTENANT JAMES ———, *SGC Course*

" I'm going into the Guards. I came here from Durham University where I read politics. I had glandular fever throughout my first term and was Y-Listed, so effectively backtermed. In RCB you spend your time thinking "What on earth are they looking for?" You can't really prepare for it, all you can do is your best. The logic tests I didn't understand at all. I immensely enjoyed the command tasks, but I was sure that I'd failed. When I was interviewed by a brigadier he said "Going off to university — Oxbridge?" and I said "No sir, Durham." "Durham? That's one of those good ones, isn't it?" I thought that rather amusing. He gave me the impression he thought that at university there'd be no politics and we'd all be wandering around in tweed suits. I didn't do a Brigade Squad, which I'd have liked to have done. It would have stood me in good stead to know what soldiers go through.

Sandhurst has been a disappointment to me, although it's good in some ways. It's a culture shock when you leave university, even if you know quite a bit about the regular Army outside. I expected it to be thoroughly enjoyable but hard work, and to be a place I could be immensely proud of. Tradition means a lot to me, and loyalty matters a lot to any soldier. To have a loyalty to Sandhurst is unfortunately very difficult. Company and platoon loyalty is very easy as you're totally interdependent — if you don't work together you just won't exist, so you form extraordinarily tight and intimate bonds between people who may have totally different interests and backgrounds and be going in different directions. But the Academy is resented, certainly in the first term. Coming back, people were pleased to see their comrades in strife but by no means proud to be walking back through the gates, or to have a Sandhurst tie. Outside, my friends working in London either have a rose-coloured picture of the Army or they think you're crazy; that if you have any brains you ought to be out earning more money or doing a job more functional to the economy.

The smallest things of all niggle you most. On a show parade we were practically taught how to frown, we had to show "smile removed from face". It was just one of those "embuggerance factors" of Sandhurst, one of the funniest and most extraordinarily ridiculous things I've ever done. Even when you're being mucked about there are laughs. The most difficult thing is lack of sleep. You're under constant pressure to keep up with your studies, which to us seems the most important thing as we've very green and when we leave we want to know what to do with our men in the field. At the same time every day we have to make sure our kit is a hundred per cent on the ball.

Sometimes there's a conflict between drill and turnout and working towards your exams. I don't know which is more important because I've yet to understand what the absolute aim of Sandhurst is. If it's to develop leadership I'm not the best person to judge how that's done. The British Army has shown in the

'Sandhurst has been a disappointment to me, although it's good in some ways.'

past that it's one of the most disciplined, and that achieves success in battle. As for flexibility, initiative and imagination, I sometimes wonder if that is not in fact suppressed here. Certainly I think it must be nearly as difficult for colour sergeants to relate to us who think as graduates as for us to understand the madness behind the crazy things we have to do. You learn very quicky that you don't explain your actions because you're not paid to think while you're here. But if you're out in the field and you don't think you're going to get an earful.

Ideally I'd have liked to have gone straight from school to SMC, as I wouldn't have found the change particularly difficult, and then perhaps go to university. One becomes confused going from university back to what is almost schooling. And it must be difficult for the DS, who don't have degrees, to relate to us. SMC have much more fun, partly because of their age. A lot of graduates are almost complacent about getting a commission, they hold a probationary one when they arrive. We have more prestige, but a lot of emphasis is put on us to do well. We're pressured to believe we're better than SMC.

I think it's important for an officer to command soldiers, men with a totally different upbringing, education and background and probably of a totally different intellect as well. He would benefit from knowing what they go through, serving alongside soldiers going into the ranks, and at the same time learn the

## STANDARD GRADUATE COURSE

| TERM | PHASE | WEEK | CONTENT | SUBJECTS COMMON TO ALL PHASES |
|---|---|---|---|---|
| **1** | **1** | 1 | Introduction to Arms and Services | Leadership |
| | | 2 | Organisation of the rifle company and platoon | |
| | | 3 | | |
| | | 4 | | |
| | **2** | 5 | LEADERSHIP/ENDURANCE EXERCISE | Map Reading |
| | | 6 | Basic Tactics. | |
| | | 7 | | |
| | | 8 | Characteristics of Armour and Artillery. | Skill at Arms |
| | | 9 | Attack, Defence and Withdrawal. | |
| | | 10 | Demolition Guards. | |
| | | 11 | | Signals |
| | | 12 | Section and platoon tactics. | |
| | | 13 | SENNYBRIDGE EXERCISE | |
| | | 14 | | Adventurous Training |
| **2** | **3** | 15 | | |
| | | 16 | Counter Revolutionary Warfare. | |
| | | 17 | | Drill |
| | | 18 | LONGMOOR (Counter revolutionary warfare exercise) | |
| | | 19 | | Physical Training |
| | | 20 | All Arms Tactics. | |
| | | 21 | | |
| | | 22 | SALISBURY PLAIN EXERCISE | Professional Academic Studies |
| | **4** | 23 | | |
| | | 24 | | |
| | | 25 | | |
| | | 26 | OVERSEAS TRAINING | |
| | | 27 | | Administration |
| | | 28 | SOVEREIGN'S PARADE | |

basic tactics they teach here. A "Sandhurst type" platoon is nothing like being an ordinary soldier. If we all trained first as soldiers perhaps we'd realize what our soldiers feel, we'd understand them better and be better officers. Training as an officer would follow after you'd been confirmed in your qualities of leadership.

I'd like to know if there is a DS "pink" [i.e., official manual] aim for Sandhurst. "Serve To Lead" — is that the aim, and if so does the training that we do stick to it? It must be difficult to achieve when the actual course-content is continually changing, so much of so many different things, trying to do so much: making us reasonable tacticians, leaders, administrators, not sticking to one aim. The cuts in the Academics are quite a shame. I believe very strongly we ought to understand what our job is about. Training suggests that if people are firing at you then you fire back, but it's important we don't become mere servants of the authorities above but understand who we're serving, who we're defending and what we're here to do. The course tries to cover the basics, but while all the other academies round the world are taking on more Academics we're cutting back. We need to be able to explain what we're doing in the Army. A lot of the graduates here, who don't have a political education, would have difficulty convincing the public that their job was in any way worth while.

Our function is to serve the Queen and the government. We're not aligned to any political persuasion. However, we obviously have some moral codes of conduct towards war which are an individual responsibility. In the last resort you have to judge the situation for yourself.

The whole course is difficult, particularly if you've no military experience before. The most difficult thing is having so many things to cope with all at once. As a young officer you'll have an immense number of responsibilities so you've got to be used to pressure. But any of us might be going to Northern Ireland, and some of the lessons of tactics needed would be better learned if we didn't have to worry so much about drill and standards of turnout, although I fully appreciate that they are essential in learning discipline and attention to detail. I'd like a longer course with higher standards in basic tactics and the same standards of drill, but that may not be cost-effective.

Anyone can get through this course, the thing to tell yourself is not to get disheartened. Sandhurst is not the Army, and what you'll be doing here is not what you'll be doing the rest of your life. It's a testing-ground you should get through if you keep your head down and show determination. It's a very short course, and they have to pick out the weak people very quickly, so it's impossible for them not to judge you on your first appointment. If you perform badly at the start you may be labelled for more pressure to come throughout the whole course. With that plus normal pressure nearly anyone will do badly, perhaps be backtermed. Others can have a lot of luck, perform well at the beginning and do well. Some high-flyers here have told me that if they'd come under pressure early they too would have made a complete muck-up of it all. You wonder if it's a fair system. Luck is a very big thing here, very big indeed. **"**

**'We need to be able to explain what we're doing in the Army.'**

*The Observer*, 13 March 1983.

JULIAN —————, *twenty-three years old, completed SGC Course 1987, Arabic speaker (degree from School of Oriental Studies, London University, going to Intelligence Corps).*

" I can't remember much that I enjoyed, except for the last exercise because we got a very coherent spirit, and the counter-insurgency exercise is very good. The first term was very boring as I'd done it all at OTC. The second term was extremely hard work. It boosts your confidence, you feel if you can handle that you can handle anything, but they screw you around tremendously. We actually asked if the timetable was deliberately mucked about. It's so haphazard. The night before the final exercise they realized that we'd been doing so much drill that they'd completely forgotten to teach us simple things like a "fix and destroy". That was the meat of the final exercise and they taught it to us in ten minutes the night before. What an outsider sees of your course is that one pass-off parade and that's why you do so much drill towards it.

Because they try to make you do so much, people learn the art of dodging and skiving. Several friends of mine (some of whom are now in Northern Ireland) are worried because all they really learned was to dodge and weave and skive out of things. I think they do try desperately hard to teach you what it's like to be in charge, but I felt horribly ill-equipped to actually lead because I'd spent most of my time either half asleep — or totally asleep — in lectures or just dodging command appointments. I think when I get there I'll be able to do the job, but I still have doubts. I don't really know what I learned at Sandhurst, you're just in a sort of daze the whole time.

It's largely a family thing [joining the Army]. It was sufficiently different from finding a job that anyone could do, walking in and out of the same office. Now I realize that you don't have to join the Army to do something different. If you're the sort of person who enjoyed boarding-school you would love the Army. There's a certain type of person whom the Army fits like a glove. Now that they were in the Army they were going to play sport and go out with the boys on the beer and talk about women. There are opinions which one couldn't express, they wouldn't be acceptable. Political ones. For example, you couldn't say you thought the Royal Family were a bag of tits! I would like to think that you could have an Army where people thought more, but then again it's not just the Army that's at fault. In the end the Army knows it can rely on a certain bedrock of person to go through. I don't think it sees any great need to change.

We had a forum in which our company commander tried hard to answer all the questions we were asked to write down, and one of them was about working wives; women who want careers. The interesting thing was that he couldn't answer it. His answer was, "Well, marry the right woman." My girlfriend has an absolute horror of being an Army wife and being lumbered with flower-arranging and wives' socials.

I am an intelligent person; why am I spending two hours every night in a red track-suit shining my boots; why am I standing here at ten o'clock at night showing dust-removed-from-forehead cap peaks? I could go off and get a job

**'There's a certain type of person whom the Army fits like a glove.'**

which didn't demand such ridiculous things of me. I think the tragedy is that at the end of the day you don't say, as you did when you began, "Well, if I had my way I'd change this," you actually find yourself saying — make it worse for the next lot, we had to do it. I think it just reflects the public-school system. Walking into the SMC bar listening to the things they talked about was just like walking into my sixth form bar at school. I don't know what the percentages are. But let's face it; Sandhurst is run by the Guards and the Guards still go back to public-school boys. It's just like stepping from one school into another — it really is no different.

'Let's face it: Sandhurst is run by the Guards.'

In university you are taught, or they attempt to teach you, to think — to reason and argue and not to accept but to question in the best possible sense. You get to Sandhurst and the first thing you're told is not to question, is to do exactly as you're told, and it's a tremendous culture shock. You get extremely fed up with it to the extent that your last refuge, really, is in the academics where you are at last allowed to think for yourself. There is a lovely story — when we got our first academic session after five weeks of pure bullshit — this character sat there, and of course he was a totally unmilitary person. We were all sitting ramrod straight in our chairs, as we had been scared stupid for the first five weeks of everybody who had come near us. He took down our surnames and then he said, "Well, what are your Christian names?" He asked the first fellow, and the guy looked blankly at him and said for a joke, "524180". But it was quite true — we hadn't had Christian names up to then. When we spoke to each other in front of the staff we had to use surnames. We weren't allowed to call each other by our Christian names.

When you're made a platoon sergeant if you don't shout a lot you're not doing your job. Just suggest that things get done and things normally do get done — but I was told off for not shouting enough, for not having enough "grip". They didn't realize that perhaps I didn't need to shout. We all found that one of the worst experiences was bayonet drill, because we were on our finger-tips in a press-up position, inches off the ground, screaming "Kill, kill, kill — kill, kill, kill" until we couldn't scream any more because we had no voice left. The character picked on me and shouted at me — he stood inches away and the spit was going all over my mouth, into my mouth from his, not very nice. He called me a fanny and a wimp because I wasn't shouting loud enough. It was degrading, really, because as an intelligent person you don't really motivate yourself like that and we found it very hard to take seriously.

Can I please say that I have never met such a bunch of collective megalomaniac sheep in my life? One skill-at-arms instructor on his own is fine, two is dodgy, and any more than two they turn into utter megalomaniacs. They screamed at us until they were blue in the face because they hate graduates and they hate officer cadets and they hate anybody but themselves and they hate anybody but the infantry. By this stage we were near enough the end of the course to laugh at them, but we were careful about it. They made our lives really miserable. I found them dreadful people, I really did.

I think what made it such hard work was the utter freedom of thought, of movement, of picking and choosing your friends, that comes with being at university and then going into such a narrow, restricted environment. I came into my own towards the end of it, when we were allowed a bit of room to manœuvre, as the company joker, the man who stands up and makes the funny speeches. I was allowed to do that, and that was quite nice. In the end we were all very sad to leave, but more so leaving the people than the place. I don't think that anyone was actually sad to leave Sandhurst: I made some extremely good friends. And the metamorphosis of members of staff is quite extraordinary from utter animal monsters when you first get there to human beings at the end of it.

I expected to see more of the class structure than I did, from the Cavalry and Guards. No one ever looked down his nose at someone else, which was a nice thing to see. But the nature of the Army bows to the system — it probably is a class-conscious system. For our final meal all the royalty were in the one dining-room with the Guards and Cavalry and a few girls and nobody else, the rest of us were in other dining-rooms with nobody interesting at all. It just showed the pecking order. But you must understand the pecking order when you join, because it won't change. The Army will, but the Guards won't. The old-boy network is still rife, the Guards will take the people they want to take, and they will never take certain people, I'm quite convinced of that.

The technical arms are always very well subscribed, and, from a soldier's point of view the Catering Corps is tremendously important because they get such good qualifications. But my guess is that the City is moving fast enough now that people just can't afford to take three years in the Guards, and then go into the City. They've got to get in straight away. I know people in the Guards who are now pledged that they will be out within a year and a half to go straight down the City. They only did it to say they'd done it — to meet a few people and see a few places. Really they're wasting their own time and the Army's.

> 'My guess is that the City is moving fast enough now that people just can't afford to take three years in the Guards, and then go into the City.'

The graduates definitely feel the odd ones out. Because the girls eat with the non-graduates they tend to mix a lot more with them, so we don't even see them. It seems to us that the mainstream of Sandhurst is still the SMC and that graduates are — well, perhaps they'll do all right when they've finished. I think the first general who is a graduate has just been through. All the permanent staff poke fun at the graduates for having so many qualifications but being unable to strip their weapons down. They might feel slightly threatened — I don't think they really need to because the job is completely different, it's a job that doesn't require education really. You don't need much of an education to be an infantry officer. It's probably why a lot of graduates get disillusioned with it, because really they're not using eighty per cent of their brain most of the time.

At the end of it, the one thing I came away with which they didn't actually teach me, but which came through, was determination. But I was quite determined before I did it. It taught me a bit of patience, and it taught me to value my free time enormously. I'll leave you a little parable. They say they're teaching you leadership through infantry tactics. One particular character of ours, he was going to be backtermed or not on one set of orders he was giving, and our sergeant admitted to us later that he did help him with his orders. All the brass appeared to watch him talk us through his model in a classroom. Now, I don't understand exactly what that's got to do with leadership? Conversely, one of the most testing leadership examples I saw was on a five-day exercise, it was pouring with rain, we'd been out there four days with no sleep at all, no nothing, we were all in gas suits, utterly pissed off, and we'd been digging and digging. And they pulled us out for a work party, led us to the top of a hill and told one character "There you go, put up three hundred yards of barbed wire with that team." And there wasn't one person there who would have done it for anything — love nor money nor nothing. And this character had to motivate us to make us do it. He bullied, he coaxed, everybody had to be treated differently. And that to my mind was real leadership. And there wasn't a single person there to take notes — it wasn't considered by them as a case of leadership at all. The real tests of leadership, like that, were completely missed.

If they say "Lead that platoon attack," it's not really leadership. They criticized vastly one of our number because he changed his direction as he came out of the helicopter, and decided he was going to go right instead of left. That's a tactical decision, it's nothing to do with leadership. And he got a very bad report from them. It flabbergasted me, because we would have all followed him anyway; we had to, I mean I'm not going to hang back if I'm being watched by the Directing Staff because that makes me look bad. The leadership is things that to a large extent I don't think they actually notice. Characters got through in our platoon who were extremely unpopular, who showed no signs of leadership at all, no character, no charisma, no nothing, and they were only noticed when we pointed it out to the directing staff.

The photos and the plaque will go on the wall saying "Well done, you did it." I've never, ever, considered doing it again. I'm glad I did it. I might not be a good person to quote because I didn't really know if I wanted to join the Army at all by the time I got to Sandhurst. For the first fourteen weeks the only thing I learned which I had not done before was how to turn on a computer. In the next fourteen weeks I learned all sorts of things about tactics which I didn't really need to know and which they readily accepted I would forget. I enjoyed the last few days. I enjoyed the friendships I made there, and the social functions, and the academics. But really it's an experience I endured rather than enjoyed. **"**

**'I might not be a good person to quote.'**

**SECOND LIEUTENANT RICHARD ———**, *SGC Course*
**"** I'm twenty-one years old, I've been here just over nine months, having been backtermed. I'm going to make it this time if it kills me. I was deputy head boy in a large comprehensive school in South Wales, then read Chemistry and Management Science at the University of Kent. I decided to join the Army in my third year and went through pre-RCB and RCB. I'm hoping to go to the Royal Corps of Transport.

Sandhurst is like no other place on earth. It's a combination of looking back at the past and at what life should be now. It's so regimented, so disciplined, a completely different way of life for me. I found it difficult in the first few months because I had absolutely no military experience and my brain just wasn't thinking in the right way. If somebody said something to me my brain said "Why?" not "How high?" as it should have. As a graduate I find Sandhurst nice but I can behave to a certain standard anyway. For some people although it's hard here it is perhaps an easy way out. You're looked after, you know your food's going to be there, somebody will be telling you what to do, you know what's happening to you. Outside you're on your own. There is an added sense of security in here.

The "pink" says that the system tries to sort out the people who've been sent here to see if they're of a standard of character and leadership to command people in war. It's very difficult to test that. You can't come up with a real situation to see if they flap and run away, whether they'll just worry about themselves or whether they'll be able to look after a group. What the SGC actually does is bring people in of all levels of skill and military experience, and the first five weeks is a big mixing pot, under a lot of pressure, trying to bind us together as a team. At the end of that five weeks those with no previous military experience can't really remember any of it and are scrabbling for what they've actually got out of it. Then the testing begins. If you're unlucky enough to be seen as a little bit shaky, then next time you're given a very testing appointment. If you dip out on that one you're given a good thrashing and put on a warning. So if you make a couple of mistakes early on, the eye is on you and you've virtually had it. But if you can be a "grey man" you can slip through here without anyone really knowing you were here.

'But if you can be a "grey man" you can slip through here.'

I think the eye fell upon me, and the heavy appointments followed. I could see them coming up, did my best, but it wasn't quite up to standard. Although I was disappointed I think it was good that I was backtermed, as I'm much more confident in command situations. Last time I really didn't know what I was doing. But backterming people puts them in with a new platoon at a late stage, and there is prejudice against them from the beginning. A system whereby remedial help was offered as people were going along, with backterming as a reserve, would be better.

Looking back on the whole course I only remember the good times, so I have enjoyed it. I don't think you'd learn as much about yourself anywhere else. Perhaps you'd have to be at war or in prison to learn as much — forced together in pressure situations, deprived of sleep, you learn whether you can cope. Some of the tactical exercises, if I'd known about them, I would have said "I know there's no way I can do that", but getting back here I can say "My God, I did that!" and you feel great about it. There's more to me than I thought there was, perhaps.

I don't know whether the system is trying to alter my behaviour outside working hours but it certainly does. Up until the age of sixteen if anyone had said I'd have to go into the Army I'd have run a mile, but I suddenly decided I'd like to join. I arrived here with virtually no civilian clothes, which was a blessing as I didn't have to iron them. But on my first leave I didn't go straight for my jeans and t-shirts. I went and bought the Army kit, the brogues, the brown cords, the Barbour coat, just to blend into the background. I really don't know why I did it. At first if I went out that's what I wore. Now perhaps I go out wearing that, but once I'm outside I put my car into a lay-by and put my jeans and sweatshirt on.

Sandhurst does mould you into a certain way of thinking, speaking and behaving. I found a big difference with my friends when I went home on leave. Their habits and behaviour made me think "My God, they shouldn't be doing that." It didn't matter to them if they listened to me or not, and that really enraged me inside, I wanted to be able to tell them and they would do it. You're the most militarized you ever are in your life in the first few weeks here. You go Army-barmy, especially those who've never done it before. You soften up a bit towards the end. My friends treated me a bit different to begin with, but now they just treat me as they always have. They're very long-standing friends and I'm really just the same underneath. I did have a girlfriend up to last weekend, but I had the "dear John" letter. There's a lot of those going around, it's very difficult having to be away.

I used to hate drill intensely because we had so much of it and I'm not very good at it. Now I enjoy it, especially with the band to march to, keeping my chin up and my back straight and being proud of what I'm doing. "Look at me, I can do it." I think we get around seventy periods of drill, with extra bits and pieces; that's too much really. It's always one company competing against another, and whoever's the worst the CSM gets shouted at and it's extra drill in the morning. It's odd but traditional, and one of the things that holds the Army together, that we're given a grant of about £1200 to spend on service dress and mess kit. Wouldn't it be better to spend that on improved combat kit than on uniforms for playing rugby in the mess at three in the morning? A lot of boys have splashed out on buying their own equipment, which we use on exercises now.

Margaret Thatcher reviews the Sovereign's Parade, 11 April 1980, (*Keystone*).

The academic side of the course has been cut down a lot this year. In my first SMG I did a course on guided missiles, and as my degree is in science I found that really interesting. That Military Technology course was excellent; it's a pity it's been dropped. War Studies is basically a history course and pretty useless now: it's not good enough to keep those who've done history interested, but it's too much for the people who haven't done history since they were thirteen, it comes too thick and fast. The Communications course is excellent, they should have more of it. We do interviews in front of a TV camera, officer/soldier interviews and so on.

'The Communications course is excellent, they should have more of it.'

We're the last course to use the SLR [Self Loading Rifle] for skill-at-arms. It's quite a good course, but again there's no remedial course. If your weapons-handling skills aren't very good you know you'll panic a bit, get shouted at, and so panic a bit more. They should perhaps try to come up with something other than the Sovereign's Parade, which would save a lot of drill periods. But I'm sure all the Guardsmen would have a heart attack if anyone suggested that. Signals Training should have more practical tests. Sometimes a whole exercise falls to bits because people just aren't up on their signals. There are also people who've slipped through the net on map-reading. They've got to a stage now where if they were put in charge of a recce they wouldn't be able to do it. If you say "I don't understand, help me" the ball is in the air whether you'll be helped correctly or picked up and backtermed, so there's something to be said for being a "grey man" trying not to be noticed. But then it means that you don't get any early command appointments. Then suddenly you get round to some hard exercise, get hammered for one of the big appointments, and you've had no experience so you've virtually had it. It's what happened to me.

My university had no OTC and I hadn't mixed with Army types before. In my mind Sandhurst was perhaps a wonderland. I expected getting up early in the morning and the whole Academy going for a run with the general at the front. What I think it is really is a sausage factory. We go through a series of tests that have been the same for the last ten or twenty years. Any changes have been additions, except for this course when they took away the Academics. As technology advanced anything extra that had come up had been pushed into the course somewhere and nothing taken out to make way for it. The whole course needs uprooting and starting from scratch again. I'm not sure about combining graduates and non-graduates. There's quite a lot of rivalry between us.

I think I have changed in status by becoming an Army officer. I don't know what it is but I feel more important with a pip on my shoulder. The best way to join the Army as an officer is to do Welbeck, the SMC, and do a technical degree while being paid as a second lieutenant. On a short-service commission I think I can get a lot more out of the Army than the Army can get out of me. When I leave after three years my job-pulling power will be a lot greater than if I'd been in the City or something else. If I find the Army good I may stay on, but that's not my intention. I want to leave at twenty-four, go into a civilian transport company and by about thirty set up my own business. **"**

*The Sunday Telegraph,*
16 March 1980.

# For Queen and country. And self.

Improper though it may sound, there's nothing wrong with a young man joining the Army for selfish as well as patriotic reasons.

Many young men look on it, not as a career in itself, but as a starting block for a career in commerce or industry.

It doesn't offend us. In fact, we consider it one of the best reasons for becoming a Short Service Commissioned Officer.

And in case you're wondering, this isn't at odds with our age-old Army principles. We'll still demand unswerving loyalty to your Monarch, your country and your regiment.

But in doing your duty you'll also be doing yourself a favour.

As a young Army Officer you'll be responsible for up to thirty men: their training, efficiency, morale and, sooner or later, their conduct when fired on by an enemy or pelted by a mob.

Make no mistake, you'll need more than a pip on your shoulder.

You'll have to be quick-witted, well-educated, hardy and approachable to gain the esteem and trust of your men.

As in the factory or office, to get results you'll have to lead, not push.

There is a difference, however. In the Army you'll be responsible for lives, not just livelihoods, so we have to make sure you're up to the job before we let you in.

In a series of interviews and tests spread over three days, you will be given every chance to make a good impression.

Then on to Sandhurst for seven months where we prove that leaders are made rather than born.

Thereafter, the regiment of your choice.

Which one depends on your qualifications and interests.

But here again you'll get the kind of leg-up any young man would envy.

Engineering, computers, accountancy or whatever: we can offer you equipment, facilities and opportunities not always available in civilian life.

They used to say that the Army would make a man of you.

Nowadays it would be equally true to say it could make a businessman of you.

A booklet we've written explains in some detail what we expect of our Officers and what they can expect from us.

It's called 'Army Officer. What the job is like and how you can apply for it.'

It sets out all the options, the different Arms and Services, the various lengths of commissions and how you may extend them or convert to a Regular Commission.

If you'd like a copy and you are between 17½ and 26 with at least 5 'O' levels including English Language, write to Major John Floyd, Dept A42, Army Officer Entry, Lansdowne House, Berkeley Square, London W1X 6AA.

### A 3-year Commission in the Army.

# WOMEN'S ROYAL ARMY CORPS

### CAPTAIN DIANE FOSTER WRAC

❝ I'm a platoon commander and instructor in the WRAC wing. I'm thirty-three years old and I've been at Sandhurst since January 1986. The Academy has a worldwide reputation which it's very anxious to preserve. It really tries very hard to live up to the ideals which the public, the Army, and indeed the world expects of it. But the image that the public probably has of Sandhurst is of very upper-crust officers with private incomes who come via public schools from very privileged backgrounds, and of course that is not the case. Three-quarters of the WRAC cadets come from the State sector, compared to about half the numbers on the SMC. One of our success stories is that 27-year-old graduates get on perfectly well with 18-year-old nongraduates. I'm quite frankly not certain what the argument is for not mixing the SGC and SMC courses. Certainly the girls are more motivated, but that's part of being a woman in a military environment. You've got to be motivated in order to survive, because it's still a male-dominated society. These are very awe-inspiring surroundings for all of us, students and DS, but whether the women are more aware of that I don't know.

> 'These are very awe-inspiring surroundings for all of us.'

It is an unusual vocation for a woman. Certainly when I joined the Army I had some very strange comments, ranging from the facetious to the obscene, on why I wanted to join. It doesn't affect the way I teach the girls. It might cause them to drift away from some of their civilian friends purely because they spend so much time with the Army — this isn't a nine-to-five job. One or two girls have arrived here with civilian boyfriends who simply haven't been able to understand or accept the restrictions that the Army environment places upon them. As a result that kind of relationship has tended to fizzle out, and the girls have made new men friends among the students here. Accommodation here is single-sex, men's out of bounds to women and vice versa, and anyone who transgresses those rules is severely dealt with. But after the first five weeks there's no reason why they can't disappear into some hotel five miles away and spend the night together. Certainly we've no objections. If a friendship is not strong it's going to disappear because of the difference in attitude and lifestyle. You work very much in a male-dominated environment and the chances are that you are going to meet Mr Right. There are still quite a few women who put their career first, and the most vociferous about that tend to be those who get engaged first!

You can't remain in the WRAC if you're pregnant. You have to leave and have your child. It's possible to be a mother and still serve in the Army, but MoD rules are that you have to convince them that the child is being properly looked after, which in practical terms means a full-time nanny. I don't know of any cases in which that has happened. Unlike many foreign armies, we have no statutory right to have a child and then serve on.

There is the idea here that the platoon commander is God, and we have a very large say as to whether they make it through the course or not. Having said that, many students are of a very similar background to us, with similar outlooks and interests. Although during the course there's very much a teacher-and-student relationship, with Army discipline thrown in as well, towards the end the relationship starts to shift, and whether you like it or not it becomes a lot more informal. We go out on adventure training with the girls and sleep in the same tents. It's hard to retain the officer-and-student relationship when they see you with mascara all over your face and your hair down in your eyes.

The girls that come in here are not people who want to sit behind a desk and look pretty, they wouldn't be in this job if they did. But because of their role in the Army they are not going to be out in the field directing troops, building bridges and going to war. It is important, because they are serving with the male Army, that they understand what is going on, and that's one of the reasons they do so much tactics here. But certainly a lot of them think "This is one of the few occasions in our career when we are going to have a big chunk of life going out, getting mucky and enjoying ourselves." And that's one of the reasons why they're so keen and enthusiastic while they're here, because they know that it won't last for ever. I'd like to see the girls atually go on exercise with the men.

In the early stages of the course there are problems of adjustment, particularly

## WRAC COURSE STRUCTURE (Women's Standard Course from September 1987)

| TERM | PHASE | WEEK | CONTENT | SUBJECTS COMMON TO ALL PHASES |
|---|---|---|---|---|
| 1 | 1 | 1 | Introduction to Arms and Organisations | Leadership |
| | | 2 | Organisation of the rifle company and platoon | |
| | | 3 | BASIC FIELD CRAFT/LEADERSHIP EXERCISE | Skill at Arms |
| | | 4 | Basic Tactics. | |
| | | 5 | | |
| | | 6 | Section and platoon battlecraft. | |
| | | 7 | Map reading. | |
| | | 8 | | |
| | 2 | 9 | LEADERSHIP/ENDURANCE EXERCISE | Signals |
| | | 10 | | |
| | | 11 | | Drill |
| | | 12 | Teaching Practices. | |
| | | 13 | OFFICE ADMINISTRATION EXERCISE | Physical |
| | | 14 | NBC. | Training |
| 2 | | 15 | | Games |
| | | 16 | | |
| | | 17 | UELTYWYN ADVENTUROUS TRAINING | Professional |
| | | 18 | | Academic |
| | | 19 | | Studies |
| | | 20 | | |
| | | 21 | Teaching Practices. | |
| | | 22 | LEADERSHIP/PATROLS EXERCISE | |
| | | 23 | | Administration |
| | | 24 | | |
| | 4 | 25 | Written Examinations. | |
| | | 26 | FINAL EXERCISE OFFICE/BROWNDOWN | Special to Arm |
| | | 27 | | Subjects |
| | | 28 | SOVEREIGN'S PARADE | |

for the girl who hasn't come from any form of Army background, or even an OTC background. Inevitably we have a lot of rules and regulations which some of the girls think are petty. Homesickness in the early days, even for girls of twenty-four or twenty-five, is sometimes a problem. We do get the odd difficulty when a girl with a civilian boyfriend gets upset as the relationship breaks up. Apart from that we don't have many problems. The girls are highly motivated, they've decided that they do want a career, and so they're prepared to put up with the side of training here that they personally don't like for the sake of a commission.

The mainstream girls here are going to be administrators, and so in contrast to the men's course our commissioning course is partly special-to-arm. That's why we teach them so much about records, service writing, military law, because these are the things they will be expected to know about from the moment they leave Sandhurst. They are more immediately employable than the men, and are generally highly regarded. Sometimes they can dig a little bit of a hole for themselves, because once people realize they have a girl on their hands who is a pretty slick operator on the paperwork side they tend to say, "Right, carry on! the men can go to war and you can stay in the office and look after this." Sometimes the girls don't like it.

'They are more immediately employable than the men.'

With the syllabus we've got at the moment the girls are as much integrated as they can be on the tactics side, and boys are really not taught the special-to-arms side, so it would be hard to integrate that. It would be hard on the physical side, because with the best will in the world the girls do not have the same strength or physical attributes.

Any training establishment has got to be top-heavy on chiefs, which the students don't often realize. They should be feeling extremely lucky that the staff-student ratio is so good. It's difficult for me to comment about the upper levels because my job is down at the sharp end. Outside a captain is a bigger cog in a smaller machine; here it's the other way around. That's just the way the system operates, and you have to accept it. But although we are outnumbered by the hierarchy, as far as the students are concerned we are the ones that are important, not them.

Teaching them to be "officers and ladies" is a delicate area, because you don't wish to sound patronizing or give offence. It would be awful if I gave the girls a lesson on how to hold a knife and fork! We assume they know how to do it, and if we see someone who doesn't then we might perhaps have a quiet word with them and explain what's done. What we do is tell them that socializing is extremely important, and run through some of the things that not many of them will have come across before: things like dress, because we are expected to dress to a certain standard. You can't go around in punk-rock clothes and still be seen as an officer: the Army wouldn't tolerate it, society wouldn't tolerate it, and most importantly your soldiers wouldn't tolerate it. Soldiers still have a fairly stereotyped view of what officers should be and it's the duty of officers to go a certain way in that direction.

The relationship between officers and soldiers is definitely changing in the more technical trades, but in the less technical trades — that of the infantryman, for example — it still remains exactly what it was before. The Army retains total control over its own social structure, but it doesn't have much control over technological evolution, and sometimes there's a conflict between the old structure and the new technology. This causes a vast amount of difficulty, and I'm not sure how the Army's going to get over it. But it doesn't affect the way we teach our cadets.

Sandhurst has its own list of leadership characteristics, and we would expect the ladies we commission to have most if not all of them: courage, integrity, enthusiasm, initiative, will-power, ability to communicate, fitness, pride in command, humanity. Here we teach the functional side, what a leader has to do in command. We look at how the girls perform in a group, and in the course each of the girls will have some position of authority. Can they communicate, control people, keep the momentum going, make sure everyone is being looked after, can they motivate the team? Also we look at how they fit into a social framework. We like to have good mixers; obvious loners are not going to be happy in the Army. The "Adair model" (see p. 112) of leadership which we use gives the students a framework to fall back on if they get into trouble.

Women tend to make better paper-workers. That's not a sexist remark, it's just that women have a better eye for detail and are happier behind a desk. The girls we commission bring a modicum of order to the "paper war", and the Army in peacetime relies on a lot of paper. Also, the WRAC motto is "Gentle in Manner, Resolute in Deed", and if they can bring a certain amount of compassion and humanity into situations outside then I feel my job hasn't been wasted. If someone objected to having a door opened for her I'd take her aside and have a word with her. We don't get a lot of feminists here. **"**

## WRAC OFFICER CADETS AND PROBATIONARY OFFICERS

**Anna Steele.** I'm Officer Cadet Anna Steele. I came up through the ranks of my own Corps, the Queen Alexandra's Royal Army Nursing Corps. I got through my RCB and I'm here. I'm twenty-four years old.

**Tracy Tong.** I'm Officer Cadet Tracy Tong. I came here after working for two years as an air hostess with a small charter firm. My father's a civilian pilot who learned to fly with the Fleet Air Arm. My mother's a housewife, but they're divorcing now. I'm twenty-two years old.

'I came here after working for two years as an air hostess.'

**Vanessa Hill.** I'm Second Lieutenant Vanessa Hill. I'm ancient, twenty-five years old. I studied Human Science at University College, London. Then I worked as a self-employed designer for a year, then went to Africa for a while, then worked for the Department of Trade and Industry as a consultant. I decided to join the Army last January. My father's a chartered Civil Engineer — he was in the Royal Engineers for twenty-five years. My mother's an SRN and she was in the QAs for five years. In fact, she met my father in the Army.

**Ruth Poole.** I'm Second Lieutenant Ruth Poole, twenty-seven years old. I was a teacher, an acting deputy headmistress, in junior school. I'm joining the Education Corps, keeping my hand in so I can get back to it afterwards, perhaps. My father's a Chief Inspector for the South Croydon area — middle class, well, working class basically. My mother's a housewife.

**Jacqueline Strong.** I'm Second Lieutenant Jacqueline Strong, aged twenty-three. My father's still serving with the REME. My mother was also a nurse. I read languages at Manchester Polytechnic, where I joined the OTC, which gave me a taste for the Army.

**Lucy McGowan.** I'm Officer Cadet Lucy McGowan, aged twenty-one, from Doncaster. My mother is an ex-SRN District Nurse who was in the QAs for three years, and my father's nothing to do with the Army whatsoever.

**Hill.** All the time, during our first term, we kept saying "Next week it'll be tough", and in fact they never really hit us with it. They could have driven us a lot harder and we'd have come out of it a lot fitter and a lot more proud of ourselves. If we're platoon commanders and we've got to go out with the men we've got to be as fit as them.

**Steele.** Ours is the first course to do all the tactics that the men do, and we do academics with them as well. We're supposed to be "officers and ladies" but at the same time they're trying to integrate us almost totally into the male course. There's a fair amount of exercise, a lot of practical writing, service writing, records, first aid. We do defence exercises but we don't dig trenches like the men. We do more military law than them, probably because a lot of us will become assistant adjutants.

**McGowan.** I think the Army wants, as an officer and a lady, someone who's polite, able to entertain people, and can show respect both to their peers and to those of a higher rank. Sandhurst isn't a finishing school, we don't have "how to be a lady" lessons.

**'Sandhurst isn't a finishing school.'**

**Strong.** We're all one breed here, we're all very much alike. We've been chosen because we're confident, capable of doing what they want us to do.

**Poole.** A lot of people are in awe of you when you're here. But when you get here you think "Why? What's so strange about this place?" I was born into a working-class family, so that's what I am, and I don't think I'll change. Everyone's got their strengths and weaknesses and you appreciate it, so the inter-platoon relationship becomes very strong; we all help each other. We have our tiffs and fights, but that's just community life. We're really very close to each other.

**McGowan.** Girls will never be completely integrated because we're non-combatants. We can't do everything the men can do. Attitudes would have to be changed totally to accept us, and they won't change. The Army is male-dominated.

**Poole.** I wouldn't mind filling a combatant role, I'd like to learn signals, to use a radio. But if a war did happen you'd be taken out straight away and replaced. That's why it's not worth while paying for women to be trained in all those things. There's no point in pretending that we could do the same as men. And there's the physical elements: men see women as frail, defenceless and so on.

**Tong.** We have academics with the SGC, but we go to the SMC parties! There is a difference between them, age mostly. The SMC are a lot more fun, while the SGC have got a reputation they know they've got to work very hard to keep, and that can make them a bit pompous. There's a feeling that SMC is "proper Sandhurst" and SGC is "girly Sandhurst" — which is why they put them with the WRAC! The SMC take it much less seriously.

**Steele.** One of the lads was at breakfast with the Commandant the other day, and admitted to the ADC that he was a Socialist. What a way to start breakfast!

**Strong.** I don't think being in the Army makes it more likely that you would vote Conservative. You have to be very careful about what you say and what you do, but if you can keep it to yourself you've a right to your own views.

**Poole.** If there was major unrest, and we had to take part in internal security operations, we'd do it without hesitation. The role we would have would be not to crush the political statement, but to control the security of the country, and that would be doing our job.

**Tong.** Everyone had their own personal "toughest thing" on the course. For me it was academics, I hadn't done anything since school.

**Poole.** Whatever fear you have they want it overcome. I'm petrified of heights. I can have both feet on the ground and still get vertigo. But if they know that and you can climb one rung of a ladder they'll praise you for it, and I didn't expect that from the Army. For someone who couldn't stand on a chair when I came here I've done some amazing things for myself, although in comparison with everyone else it's probably nothing.

**Hill.** We do tactics in the classroom and it all makes sense. Then they take us out and say "Right, Miss Hill, you're leading a section attack." I grab a sergeant and say "Tell me what to do!" I'm useless. It's not command, because I can "command and control" perfectly easily, it's just that I haven't a clue what to do — left flanking, or up the bank, or catch a bus, or whatever.

**Steele.** Academics is always total and utter chaos. They never know which classroom they're supposed to be in, and they may not have prepared what they're supposed to be teaching that day. If we have a military lesson you know what it's going to be, and they have a structure in front of them.

'**Academics is always total and utter chaos.**'

**Tong.** I think it's a wonderful opportunity. You can stay on as long as you like, you lead a really full life. I really do think that it's an excellent career. It's the ultimate experience, the ultimate challenge.

**Poole.** This lieutenant-colonel asked me "What are your ambitions in life?" and I said "Well, if I do join the Army I'll be a Field-Marshal by the time I'm forty." And he just looked at me, he didn't know how to take it. And then this grin spread over his face, and he said, "It's never been done, Miss", and he just laughed and laughed.

# "They told me I had 48 hours to live."

*A Kalashnikov used by the Guerrillas.*

Captain Jonathan Bailey celebrated the Christmas of 1979 in the heat of the Rhodesian bush.

He was in command of a Ceasefire Assembly Place, 300 miles from Salisbury and 5,000 miles from home.

His orders were brief and to the point.

To muster guerrillas from the bush and persuade them to remain at the Assembly Place until the Zimbabwe elections could take place in March, 1980.

Understandably, the guerrillas were highly suspicious and Bailey's first task was to gain their confidence.

Overt displays of force and weaponry were out of the question.

"The local Police, who acted as our guides, viewed us with total disbelief," he recalls.

"They had seen civil war raging in the bush for the previous eight years.

Now they were confronted by a British Army Officer and 11 men who were to enforce a ceasefire, armed only with rifles and good will.

They left with the comforting prediction that we'd probably be dead inside 48 hours."

The next day a note arrived (reprinted right) inviting Bailey to meet the guerrillas further out in the bush.

He weighed up the pros and cons and politely declined.

"I thought they were sparring with us," he says. "When we stood our ground, they had to come to us."

Five hours later the first group arrived, followed by another and another. At the end of the first week, Bailey and his men had charge of 800 guerrillas.

Then the logistical problems began.

To provide fresh water for 800 in the back of beyond, Bailey requested assistance from the Royal Engineers.

Two five thousand gallon water tanks were constructed, together with a pipeline that stretched two kilometres to the local Umfuli river.

A detachment from the Royal Army Medical Corps was also flown in. And a regular air drop of food and medicines by RAF Hercules was organised.

"On top of all this, we had to concentrate on building a relationship of trust with the guerrillas," records Bailey.

"We organised as many activities as we could think of - football, volleyball, fitness training.

I even gave a lecture on the Reformation of the Church. They seemed very interested in religion."

Even so, the ensuing months were not without their tension.

The guerrillas retained possession of their weapons throughout and guns were occasionally fired by accident.

Typically, this caused them all to prime their weapons, often firing in the air.

In March, the elections took place successfully. But Bailey is quick to deflect any praise that comes his way.

"We were sitting ducks from the word go. The fact that we survived is due entirely to the peaceful intentions of the guerrillas.

Their leader set the seal on events when he visited the Assembly Place. He told his men to vote as they pleased and to accept the outcome, whatever it might be."

## A career in the Gunners.

Jonathan Bailey applied to join the Royal Artillery after spending three years at Sussex University. (He gained an upper second in medieval history.)

He had decided not to forge any links with the Army during his time at Sussex, preferring to read for a degree under his own steam.

Sandhurst, in consequence, came as something of a shock to his system.

"I was used to a couple of lectures a day, starting at ten in the morning. Hardly a grounding for the dawn to dusk bombardment of Sandhurst.

In the end, I got my head down and concentrated on survival."

*The Note.*

*The self-propelled M110 gun, deployed in Germany.*

Survive he did, passing out as an Officer in 1973. He chose to join the Royal Artillery, primarily because of the variety of activities offered by that Regiment.

In his first four years he was a Command Post Officer, a Gun Position Officer and a Troop Commander.

He spent time in Cyprus, Northern Ireland and Germany.

Despite the need to get to grips with advanced and ever-changing weapons during this time, Bailey recalls the problems of leadership as being the most demanding.

"From day one you are responsible for the fitness, training and, ultimately, the safety of your men.

You can also find yourself doubling as a welfare officer and a marriage guidance counsellor."

Promoted to the rank of Captain, he spent the next two years back in the classroom.

First as an instructor in surveillance and intelligence techniques. Then as a student of infantry tactics and staff duties.

As Bailey points out, you rarely get bored with a job in the Army. They don't give you the time.

### War in the Falklands.

When he returned from Zimbabwe, Jonathan Bailey took up the post of Adjutant in 4 Field Regiment Royal Artillery.

In April 1982, he was deployed with the Regiment to the South Atlantic, with the rank of Major.

Given 48 hours notice, he took command of the troops on the Baltic Ferry, being responsible during the voyage for morale, discipline and battle readiness.

On arrival in the Falklands, he was to co-ordinate the fire support cell for 5 Infantry Brigade.

In plain English, to organise the shelling of Argentine positions prior to precisely timed infantry advances.

The problem for Bailey was that the shelling involved not just the Royal Artillery, but also the Royal Navy and RAF Harriers.

"We had to sit down and thrash out a co-ordinated fire plan under extremely difficult circumstances.

The movement of ships and the availability of Harriers and supply helicopters all had to be taken into account.

Then there was the weather..."

Of course, the Royal Artillery had their own problems, too. "Years of training stand you in good stead for operations like the Falklands. But even so, the sheer scale of the action caused us a few headaches.

In the last twelve hours of the battle for Port Stanley, five batteries fired the equivalent of one regiment's training ammunition for four years.

After firing three hundred rounds, it took a detachment three hours just to move the empty salvage back thirty metres behind their gun."

Looking back, Major Bailey regards his early years in the Royal Artillery, when everything was new, as the most demanding of his career.

But he recalls Zimbabwe and the Falklands as the most rewarding chapters to date.

"What appeals to me about the Army is that the unexpected always seems to happen, just when you think life is becoming routine.

Any Officer can suddenly find himself on active service with the chance to influence events, to stamp his mark.

What other career could offer as much?"

If you would like to know more about life as an Army Officer, write to Major John Floyd, Army Officer Entry, Dept. B1, Empress State Building, Lillie Road, London SW6 1TR. Tell him your date of birth, your school or university and the qualifications you have or expect.

**Army Officer**

*Four years ammunition in twelve hours...*

# THE TERRITORIAL ARMY

**TIM ——**, *Territorial Army Officer*

❝ I'm twenty-nine years old, an accountant, and I've completed the Sandhurst Territorial Officers' Course which is two weeks long. When three of us arrived in Victory College, with our suitcases under our arms, we were met by the CSM. He told the chap on my left to "fuck off out of the Academy and go and get a haircut", and the chap on my right, dressed in jeans and a t-shirt, to "fuck off into the car park and get changed into a suit". I thought this was par for the course and only to be expected. We had our documentation sorted out, had a kit issue, we were marched in civvies over to the armoury to collect weapons and had an introductory talk. It was a bit of a shock, but also expected. Really, we expected to be shocked.

The course itself was very good in many ways, very pressurized at times, with only one day off in the middle. It really finished on the Thursday afternoon of the last week, which gave the DS time to make decisions on which officer cadets had passed and failed. There was a lot of instruction, map-reading exercises, tactical exercises, a lot of demonstrations, a period in the audio-visual room giving lecturettes, command tasks, a final exercise for three days and two nights which was quite punishing, a lot of drill instruction on the square, a lot of lectures and a closing debrief.

Drill was very hard, Territorial soldiers don't often do drill except on their recruit cadres. Everybody was trying very hard but if you made the slightest mistake you were abused verbally for it. People were threatened with being placed under close arrest, although of course no one ever was. We were told right away that a very high standard of turnout would be expected of us, and it was. If you didn't meet the standard you had a show parade, which meant you had to turn out the next night at ten o'clock in your Number 2s showing the item of kit which was deficient. That gave them another chance to inspect you and they could find something else wrong. One chap put his belt buckle on and left a fingerprint, which he noticed, so he dusted it off. But he left a tiny bit of fluff from the duster on the belt buckle and that was picked up. It taught me how good the colour sergeants were at inspecting. I always swore that they were wasted, they should be scene-of-crime officers in the Metropolitan Police. No detail escaped their attention.

For TA soldiers we spent too much time on drill. We don't do ceremonial duties, and those units that do like the HAC make sure they're practised at the time. I accept that drill is a way of enforcing discipline and uniformity, which is important, but there are other ways which would have been more constructive such as field training. Doing tactical exercises instils discipline more than parade-ground drill and is more useful for TA soldiers. We spent so much time drilling rather than learning about administration in the field or tactics. It didn't help build your confidence in the way that adventure and leadership training

**'Fuck off into the car-park and get changed into a suit.'**

**Opposite:**
*The Sunday Times,* 26 February 1984.

239

does. I question whether the time was spent as usefully as it could have been, going endlessly round the square.

I was reasonably competent at most things when I arrived and better at most things I'd been taught when I left. Most of all, having been through it my confidence in my own abilities has increased. I must have something to have got through it. It is the regular Army looking at you and setting a standard for the TA which they won't drop. It means I have the right to give orders to the TA soldiers — and Regular soldiers on occasions — that I work with. I have got the Sandhurst seal of approval as a reserve officer.

There's something which isn't always appreciated by Regulars who say we're only here for a fortnight. Going back five or six years there was a very strong feeling in both the TA and the Regulars that TA officer standards weren't very high and varied a lot. Since then all officers apart from certain specialists, like doctors, have to do a District Assessment Board, which is identical to RCB, taking place over a full weekend. It starts on Friday evening with written papers, then on Saturday lecturettes, interviews, appreciations, then an obstacle course in the gym in the morning, and in the afternoon command tasks and a discussion group. On Sunday you do command tasks with leaders. The whole regime does give the Board time to assess your qualities of leadership. Also pre-Sandhurst training has been introduced to prepare us for the Sandhurst course, and all the aspirants have to get their CO's recommendation after being in the TA as soldiers for a year. So becoming a TA officer doesn't just involve signing on and turning up at Sandhurst."

**Opposite:**
The Queen at her own parade, 12 April 1985. (*Press Association*).

Princess Anne, representing the Queen at Sovereign's Parade, inspects the WRAC, 11 April 1986. (*Press Association*).

# CONCLUSION

This final chapter has proved a most difficult one to write. The tone of this conclusion is critical, but I hope readers will take my own affection for the RMAS as read. One might begin to build an overview of today's Sandhurst by identifying three basic functions: the symbolic, the social and the instructional. The symbolic and the social are closely linked, and may conflict with Sandhurst's rapidly expanding instructional function, the growth of which parallels the introduction of new technology into the Army. Sandhurst used to have a fourth educational function, but this has been drastically diminished in recent years.

## SANDHURST AS A SYMBOL

Sandhurst is an important international symbol of British power and prestige. This function has become more significant since the loss of Empire and the consequent loss of super-power status. Sandhurst is also an important symbol for the British Army itself; it represents the officer corps and a continued commitment to a commissioned and non-commissioned rank structure. This aspect of its symbolic function becomes more significant as similiar class-based divisions in the broader society are not so automatically accepted as in the past.

Despite the increasing significance of its symbolic function, and the continued allocation of resources to keep up its familiar image, the substance of Sandhurst has changed radically. Few would deny that the new pruned Sandhurst tries to achieve far less academically than did the pre-1972 Sandhurst. Any campus pretensions have gone, and with them the concept of the Army's responsibility for producing broadly educated citizen officers. The Commandant told me, 'Sandhurst can't afford to be the philanthropic organization it once was. (see p.196) Although Sandhurst can no longer afford to *be* what it once was, it still prefers to *appear* as it once was, and the maintenance and projection of the old image rather than that of the new rationalized, partially privatized,[1] OCTU can be problematic.

[1] Catering and management of the grounds have now been put out, or are about to be put out, to private contractors with the loss of many 'old retainers'. Privatization of the library and of the remaining academic departments is being considered.

**Opposite:**
The Traditional Image: Practice for the Sovereign's Parade, March 1973 (*Keystone*).

Many of the young people I spoke to at Sandhurst told me they had a very false idea of what to expect when they arrived. Part of the reason, I suspect, is the disproportionate attention which is being focused on the superficial. I am particularly critical of the work of the professional image-manipulators who gild the lily of Sandhurst's traditional image and deliberately promote a myth. There is, of course, absolutely nothing wrong in being proud of a great national institution, or encouraging others to take pride in it. The potential danger comes when perception is focused away from the real towards the illusory, and when the illusory itself interacts with and moulds an individual's reality. This leads to confusion. My main observation and criticism of today's Sandhurst is that it has become confused at a number of levels.

Confusion tends to be contagious. Being at the RMAS still confers very special status on the individual student. When he has passed the course he is labelled 'Sandhurst trained'. However, as we have noted, this does not mean as much as it once did. It means that the individual has attended a course which for most will be about half a year long. His confidence can be permanently damaged when his performance does not come up to his own expectations or those of others. Such expectations may be held at an artificially high level because the Army insists on preserving the same impressive façade as ever, reinforcing the impression that the course is far more comprehensive today than is in fact the case.

## SANDHURST AS A RITE OF PASSAGE
Just as Sandhurst's symbolic role has become more important in recent years, the function of Sandhurst as a rite of passage into the officer corps of the British Army also appears to be of growing significance to Army planners. They have stated quite specifically in the ROTE report that the officer corps of the future will be drawn from 'less traditional sources' — in other words, there will be more entrants from non-public school backgrounds, and the Army must react accordingly. They imply that State sector schools are less likely to inculcate the right leadership qualities. Within the context of the existing structure of the Army and its own definition of leadership, the Army planners may well be right. One should make it quite clear, though, that they are not trying to discourage applicants from what they term the less traditional sources. On the contrary, these young people are desperately needed to make up for the shortfalls in officer-recruiting. However, the Army believes such applicants must be socially modified 'to fit in'.

This modification entails changing the habits they have learnt from their parents and former peers towards a more middle-class template.

The Army assumes that officers produced by this process will be more respected by their men. There is little doubt that they will be more distanced from them. To quote the Commandant: 'If the soldiers begin to know their officers too well they also begin not to respect them (see p. 194)'. If one is speaking practically of today's Army, he is probably right, but one must nevertheless accept that this is a heavy indictment of the current system, as it implies that soldiers are encouraged to believe that their officers are rather more superior to them than is in fact the case. Bluntly put, they are being deceived. As soldiers themselves tend to be far better informed and educated than in the past, and are given more responsibility, the fiction that officers are god-like figures becomes ever more difficult to maintain, and the strains on the existing system grow.[2] The Special Air Service and Israel's Defence Forces have both shown that soldiers can be on closer terms with their officers without any loss of respect or efficiency. Less formal hierarchies, though, demand highly trained and crucially, self-motivated members.

Perhaps part of the problem in the British case is that middle-class officers and the class system they represent have become so deeply ingrained in the national psyche. In the Army this class system is reinforced by the regimental system, which has its origins in feudalism. It is often said by senior officers (who, one notes, have a very comfortable life within it) that the regimental system is the greatest strength of the British Army, but if it is too rigidly clung to this may become its greatest weakness. Sandhurst is geared towards the regimental system; it operates much like a regiment, and it listens very carefully to the comments of regimental commanders on its products.

One cannot deny that the current regimental system has very great strengths, but a fundamental confusion can arise between family spirit, acceptance of individuality and tradition which are fostered in the regimental system and the system itself. There are other ways wherein the former admirable qualities — which together with a unique courage and determination have been the key to many British military successes — might be fostered without maintaining outmoded, frequently bogus and blatantly unjust class prejudice. It is not a question of the destruction of the regimental system but of its natural evolution. This, it appears, is being repressed at the moment.

---

[2] A former senior instructing officer at Sandhurst noted upon reading this conclusion: 'The young sergeant of today is far better trained than in the past. He has completed courses as an instructor in a number of subjects. Inevitably soldiers compare him to their commissioned platoon commander and the latter — although he may one day make a good captain or major — does not always come off favourably. This was a problem in the past too, but, it is a greater problem today.

The whole business of a manipulated 'bourgeoisification' of working-class potential officers to fit the regimental system lacks integrity, however one may try to justify it. It can also be rather a con on the individual, who can even be at risk of psychological damage by the process. The Army may appear via Sandhurst to offer class mobility unavailable elsewhere, but the transformation is not quite perfect. There is still prejudice in the officer corps, where middle-class officers find no difficulty in recognizing those who have not been born to their class. Boys from working-class backgrounds still find it almost impossible to become officers in some regiments. Rather like Dr Faustus, the eager upwardly mobile potential officer may not get quite the deal he has been led to believe.

The rite-of-passage function of Sandhurst does not only affect students from working-class backgrounds. It is one hypothesis of this book that Sandhurst's primary function for all its students is, as it has been in the past, as a rite of passage, and that any other training is supplementary to this end. One cannot be sure whether the Army intended Sandhurst to develop in this way, but other important factors enter the equation, one being the students themselves. As a collective body, they take what they most need from the course. What is this? Principally a great deal of pride, friendship forged by shared suffering, a little military knowledge and some basic skills. Students I spoke to were unanimous that a great deal of the course went in one ear and out of the other, and some regarded it as essential in order to know what might be safely ignored without incurring the wrath of the system. Their reaction was logical and practical, considering the sometimes self-defeating intensity of the course.

## INSTRUCTION AT THE NEW SANDHURST

It has been noted earlier in this book that Sandhurst's role has become confused as the Army becomes more technologically orientated. The Sandhurst curriculum has become a pot-pourri where an attempt is made to cram a vast amount of information into students. It is accepted by instructing officers that much will not be remembered. One might ask, then, why teach that which it is expected will be forgotten? The Army's answer would probably include reference to the fact that the Sandhurst course is designed to be an introduction to many things. The emphasis, it would probably be suggested, is not on military skills or knowledge but on promoting leadership. But at other times one is told that Sandhurst offers important, potentially life-saving, training in areas which many students will never cover again. One cannot have it both ways.

Students leave Sandhurst with a range of skill levels far greater than any grading statistics might suggest. This is a real problem. Unofficially staff will tell you that standards have fallen too low, that Sandhurst is in danger of becoming a sausage factory; budgetary and time constraints leave little alternative. There must be a minimum standard even when specific training is used principally as a vehicle for teaching other things. If in truth it is not always being met, there is no choice but an extension of the course or a reduction in subjects covered.

One cannot overstress that too many students feel frustrated;[3] they complain of being permanently punch-drunk from lack of sleep and a combination of physical and psychological stress which is not conducive to learning. Of course, it is important that students be toughened up physically and mentally, but this must not be and need not be at the cost of efficient teaching. One notes the Colour Sergeant's story of the impossibility of properly teaching the vital subject of first aid in the time allotted. The standard military course has now been extended, but rather than take advantage of this and spread out the old syllabus over three terms a new and even fuller course is to be introduced. One item which might have been significantly if not drastically cut — drill — remains unchanged. In the real world is not first aid a greater priority?

## EDUCATION
In the meantime, academic education, with the exception of the limited component added to the SMC course, has been scrapped (overall, if one is looking at Regular officer education, even those young men starting their careers on SMC will have a drastic reduction in the education given them by the Army because of the replacement of the RCC course by the modified JCSC course). Can this be justified in today's ever more complex environment? I will not bore readers by repeating all that has been said in previous chapters; it is enough to note that education teaches the principles behind learning. It is universally applicable, unlike instruction. An Army officer, or indeed any soldier, obviously needs both. The Army will argue that Sandhurst students no longer require all the education that was once offered at the RMAS; civilian education, particularly in the case of the ever more common graduate entrants, covers much of the same ground. But does it? How many graduates, let alone non-graduates, are truly familiar with international affairs or the constitutional structure of the United Kingdom and its relationship to the Army? How many Army officers can speak even the most basic German (let alone Russian)? Not that many. Yet these should be familiar subjects to any would-be Army officer, as they relate even at junior level to his command decisions.

[3] This comment only applies to male students, female students, privately and publicly, were far less critical.

Advocates of the 'systems' approach might say that the system for which they are designing does not demand such knowledge in its junior managers to run efficiently. That attitude is dangerously unimaginative. One is reminded of a young officer in the Falklands who noted that it was only because of what he had learnt on the now defunct RCC course that he could properly answer the constant questions from his soldiers as to why they were there.

## LEADERSHIP

The increasing emphasis on instruction at the cost of the sort of education where the student is taught and practised in the principles to aid learning rather than force-fed information like a computer must have significant consequences. Not least is the inability to achieve the aims of instruction. Human beings in general are rather poor performers when reduced to a merely mechanical function. Many of Britain's greatest military leaders have had most unconventional backgrounds. A balance must be achieved, and reflected in officer-training, between imaginative leadership and predictable leadership. Officers need both qualities; imaginative flexible leadership is essential in battle, predictable military leadership is essential for administration. The Sandhurst course as it has developed in recent years appears to have become geared more and more towards predictable leadership. The application of the systems approach is part of this trend. Politicians, planners, bureaucrats and computers demand predictability, but it is often the serendipity factor which wins wars.

Even when one considers the Army as a peace-time organization, the systems approach or any other simplified 'scientific' model may not come up with the right answers. There are in it many good officers, gentlemen in the best sense, who although they are not themselves ambitious inspire and help others. They do so without being technical, tactical or management whiz-kids; they possess another indefinable factor, which is unrecognized by systems analysts and which might be imprecisely labelled 'human sensitivity'. It is a vital factor in any successful human system, and one which leads to more efficient management even when analysis is made in the most materialistic way if the tools of observation are subtle enough.

A peace-time Army officered by thrusting man-managers may create a marvellously efficient defence bureaucracy, but will it help win the third world war, or offer an adequate response to terrorism? It seems that the needs of the system and its maintenance have become paramount. A real quest for efficiency must consider the system itself far more radically than has been done to date. Army officers are probably not the best people to make that analysis (although of course they should contribute to it) since they have a vested interest in the current status quo and will naturally look for justifications to preserve it.

## TRADITION-BASED REFORM: THE WAY FORWARD

Some readers may feel that the current system may not be perfect but that it works in practice. One might reply that it has usually worked in the past, but there is no guarantee that it will work in the future. How might things be improved? It appears that one basic problem is cost. The Army is afraid of wasting resources on the short-service officers — the bulk of today's young officers — who may disappear in a few years and take their expensive training with them. To avoid wasting resources, one might suggest extending the short-service commission to a minimum of four years; many officers extend it as it is. In order to encourage into the Army as officers young men who are not willing to make a four-year commitment, one might also encourage more applicants for the existing short-service limited commission. Apart from those applicants coming in on the SSLC scheme, and the Chaplains and dentists and the like, all potential officers would complete six months' service in the ranks,[4] to be followed by a one-year four-term Sandhurst course. (Some senior officers at Sandhurst today, despite defending ROTE officially, will admit that a single Sandhurst course would make much better use of resources and be much easier to administer.) The first two terms could be devoted to initiation and training in basic skills (usable skills would replace drill as the *main* focus of group bonding), the second two terms to academic education but with regular practice in skill-at-arms and map-reading (I believe that competence in these two subjects is vital for an officer's confidence). Regular officers could return after four years' service with their units and complete an extra two-term academic package, and some graduates among their number might be encouraged to stay longer in order to complete a Master's degree. After the implementation of such a system any short-fall in officer-recruitment could and should be made up by increasing the number of commissions from the ranks.

My intention throughout this book has been to promote thought and discussion. Sandhurst is far too important to be considered in a romanticized haze, as it sometimes has been. Broadly speaking, I believe the RMAS has been moving in the wrong direction in recent years, but then I must make my own position clear; I believe that that is true of the whole of Britain. The relentless application of monetarist principles has made us perceive the world and our position within it in a very short-term way. We have allowed ourselves to fall into the trap

---

[4] SSLC entrants would also serve in the ranks initially, but only for a month or six weeks.

**Overleaf:**
Major V.F. Erskine Crum, Scots Guards, mounts the steps of Old College after the Sovereign's Parade in February 1954. The curious custom of riding up the steps was begun by Sandhurst's most famous adjutant 'Boy Browning' and has been continued ever since by his successors. (*Topham*).

of using grossly materialistic tools of analysis, the origins of which can be traced to Marxist dialectics. We describe ourselves now as capitalists, and the enemy are communists, but both might be considered rungs on the same ladder.

At Sandhurst today, as in the Army and industry, the quest is for increased efficiency. On paper the Sandhurst course looks extraordinarily efficient, but in practice, at the level of the individual rather than that of the system, the same cannot be said. Several students told me that they were surprised at how disorganized their training appeared to be in practice. Efficiency is important; the Army, like other large extended organizations, sometimes suffers from gross inefficiency. I can remember ammunition being fired off at the end of the financial year to ensure next year's quota! I'm told the practice continues. This sort of waste is the result of encouraging too much rigidity in the system, and whether that rigidity is efficiently streamlined by systems analysts or not makes little difference, as effort is being focused initially in the wrong place. The fundamental inefficiency remains. An obsession with systems efficiency may give unwarranted new life to a system which is beginning to fail.

There is a fundamental disequilibrium in the current system. Sandhurst's expanding social and instructional functions inevitably are coming into conflict. The maintenance of old class structures to which Sandhurst's social function relates is difficult in a world orientated to new technology. The old social system mirrored a pre-technological society and may not be the most effective way of controlling and making use of the new technology. Equally the Army's existing social structure may not be the most effective way of fighting the enemy's technology, whether or not one adopts that technology oneself. This is not a Luddite position. It is often too easily assumed that one must adopt high-tech to fight high-tech.

In the final analysis, however, the answers to defence problems cannot be found just in the application of pure logic. It will never be enough just to be more efficient than the enemy; one must retain a commitment to being more moral. It is doubtful whether there can be long-term efficiency in valid human terms without a firm moral base.

The loss of academic studies at Sandhurst is a particular tragedy. It is a sign of our vanishing commitment to our principles. Nevertheless, in spite of all the steps in the wrong direction, the essence of Sandhurst survives. Students cope with their accelerated courses and manage when they leave. There is still a great group spirit, camaraderie and sense of fun, and still young men go from Sandhurst and risk their lives for their country.

# INDEX

Figures in italic indicate an illustration.